**THE ROYAL COURT THEATRE AND
BRISTOL OLD VIC IN ASSOCIATION
WITH THE MARKET THEATRE PRESENTS**

A GOOD HOUSE

By Amy Jephta

A Good House was first performed at The Royal Court Theatre
Downstairs on Saturday 11 January 2025, then transferred to
Bristol Old Vic from Friday 14 February 2025.

A Good House

Written by Amy Jephta

Andrew **Kai Luke Brummer**
Lynette **Olivia Darnley**
Bonolo **Mimî M Khayisa**
Sihle **Sifiso Mazibuko**
Jess **Robyn Rainsford**
Christopher **Scott Sparrow**

Director **Nancy Medina**
Designer **ULTZ**
Lighting Designer **Chris Davey**
Composer **Femi Temowo**
Sound Designer **Elena Peña**
Associate Director **Tatenda Shamiso**
Casting Director **Arthur Carrington**
Modelmaking & Drawing **Mark Simmonds**
Assistant Designer **Shaquelle Devroux**
Voice and Accent Coach **Hazel Holder**
Dramatherapist **Samantha Adams**
Stage Manager **Martha Mamo**
Deputy Stage Manager **Olivia Roberts**
Assistant Stage Manager **Emily Mei-Ling Pearce**
Sound Operator **Patrick O'Sullivan**
Scenery built by **Bristol Old Vic Scenic Workshop**

From the Royal Court, on this production:
Executive Producer **Steven Atkinson**
Dramaturg **Gillian Greer**
Producing Co-ordinator **Winnie Imara**
Production Manager **Marius Rønning**
Company Manager **Mica Taylor**
Lead Producer **Ralph Thompson**
Costume Supervisor **Lucy Walshaw**
Lighting Supervisor **Lucinda Plummer**
Lighting Programmer **Lizzie Skellett**
Lighting Operator **Daisy Simmons**
Stage Supervisor **Steve Evans**
Stage Show Technician **Oscar Sale**
Stage Crew **Tom Glenister**

Originally co-commissioned by the Royal Court Theatre with the Fugard Theatre, South Africa.

The Royal Court and Stage Management wish to thank the following for their help with this production: F&A Fruits LTD

Amy Jephta (Writer)

For the Royal Court: **This Liquid Earth: A Eulogy in Verse (&Edinburgh International Festival/HighTide Festival); All Who Pass (&Grahamstown National Arts Festival; Shoes (&Carnegie Hall).**

Other theatre includes: **Kristalvlakte (Fugard/Aardklop Festival); Flight Lessons (Jermyn Street/Theatre 503/Edinburgh Fringe Festival); Free Falling Bird (Bush); Other People's Lives (Artscape); Refuge (British Council/Connect ZA), Here To There (Afrovibes Festival), Kitchen (Riksteatern, Sweden), Soldaat (Artscape).**

Samantha Adams
(Dramatherapist)

Theatre includes: **War Horse, Mnemonic, Hot Wing King, Trouble in Mind, Othello (National); Reverberations, Choir Boy (Bristol Old Vic); Machinal (Old Vic); Dr Semmelweis (Sonia Friedman Productions); The Meaning of Zong (Bristol Old Vic & Barbican).**

TV includes: **Babies, Inheritance.**

Kai Luke Brummer (Andrew)

Theatre includes: **MOFFIE (Riverside Studios); Master Harold and The Boys (The Fugard Theatre); The Curious Incident of the Dog in the Night-Time (Theatre on The Bay); When Swallows Cry (The Baxter Theatre).**

Film includes: **MOFFIE, Professionals, Eraser: Reborn, Desert Rose.**

Arthur Carrington
(Casting Director)

As casting director, for the Royal Court, theatre includes: **BRACE BRACE, Giant, ECHO, Bluets, Blue Mist, Hope has a Happy Meal, Graceland, Jews. In Their Own Words, A Fight Against...(Una Luca Contra...), Maryland, Poet in da Corner.**

As casting associate, for the Royal Court, theatre includes: **The Ferryman (& Broadway), Hangmen (& New York/West End).**

As casting director, other theatre includes: **King Troll (The Fawn/New Diorama); Paradise Lost (lies unopened beside me/ Tour); Little Deaths (Summerhall); Visit from an Unknown Woman (Hampstead); Liberation Squares (Nottingham Playhouse /Brixton House & tour); The Contingency Plan (Sheffield Crucible); Barefoot in the Park (Pitlochry Festival Theatre/Royal Lyceum); Returning to Haifa (Finborough); The Ugly One (Park); The Mountaintop (Young Vic).**

As Casting Associate, for other theatre includes: **Dr Strangelove, Waiting for Godot, Slave Play, The Hills of California (& Broadway), Lyonesse, The Pillowman, Hamnet (& RSC), Jerusalem, Leopoldstadt, Uncle Vanya, The Night of the Iguana, Rosmersholm, True West (West End); Macbeth (UK/US Tour); La Cage Aux Folles (Regents Park Open Air); Drive Your Plow Over the Bones of the Dead (Complicité/ tour); Shipwreck, Albion (Almeida); A Very, Very, Very Dark Matter (Bridge).**

Film includes: **The Unlikely Pilgrimage of Harold Fry, Maryland, Ballywalter.**

Olivia Darnley (Lynette)

Theatre includes: **A Single Man (Park); The Meeting, A Marvellous Year for Plums (Chichester Festival); Masterpieces, Accolade, The Rat Trap (Finborough); Ugly Lies The Bone (National); Twelfth Night (Filter); Wolf Hall/Bring Up The Bodies (RSC/Aldwych/Broadway); Pride and Prejudice, A Midsummer Night's Dream, Macbeth (Regent's Park Open Air); A Day In The Death of Joe Egg (Citizen's); All My Sons (Apollo); Artist Descending A Staircase (Old Red Lion); As You Like It, The Little Fir Tree (Sheffield Theatres); Hay Fever (Theatre Royal, Haymarket); Arms & The Man (Salisbury Playhouse); Much Ado About Nothing, Private Lives (Theatre Royal Bath); Northanger Abbey (Theatre Royal York), Les Liaisons (Bristol Old Vic).**

Television includes: **Doc Martin, Call The Midwife, Grantchester, Titanic, Inspector Lynley Mysteries, Agatha Christie: A Life in Pictures, Hughie Green: Most Sincerely, Doctors, Miss Marple.**

Film includes: **Benediction, Seacole, Death Defying Acts, You, Me and Him.**

Chris Davey (Lighting Designer)

For the Royal Court: **The Force of Change, Catch, The Sugar Syndrome, Crazyblackmuthafuckinself.**

Other theatre includes: **The Magic Flute (Opera North); Touching the Void (Parko Theatre Tokyo/West End); The Other Boleyn Girl (Chichester Festival); Death of England (SohoPlace); Twelve Angry Men (National Tour); Tarantino Live (Riverside Studios); And Then There Were None (National & International tour); The Gifting (Leeds Year of Culture); Noah's Flood (Slung Low/Manchester International Festival); Richard III (Rose** Theatre/Liverpool Playhouse); **42nd Street (Chatelet Theatre), Matthew Bourne's The Car Man (Royal Albert Hall); Footloose (National tour); Rhinoceros (Edinburgh International Festival); Vamos Cuba! (Sadler's Wells); Sweeney Todd (La Monnaie); Matthew Bourne's Lord of the Flies (Sadler's Wells, national and international tours); The Driver's Seat (National Theatre of Scotland); Carlos Acosta's Classical Selection (Coliseum, Royal Albert Hall and world tour).**

Shaquelle Devroux (Assistant Designer)

This is Shaquelle's debut play.

Training credits: **Genesis Theatre Design Programme.**

Hazel Holder (Voice and Dialect Coach)

For the Royal Court: **Giant, seven methods of killing kylie jenner, A Kind of People, Poet in Da Corner, Cuttin' It (& Young Vic/Birmingham Rep/Sheffield Theatres/Yard), Grimly Handsome, ear for eye, Father Comes Home from the Wars (Parts 1, 2 & 3), Pigs & Dogs.**

Other theatre includes: **The Importance of Being Earnest, A Tupperware of Ashes, The Grapes of Wrath, The Hot Wing King, People, Places & Things, Death of England Trilogy, The Effect, Grenfell: in the words of survivors, Blues for an Alabama Sky, Small Island, Trouble in Mind, Rockets and Blue Lights, Pericles, Julie, Nine Night, Barber Shop Chronicles, Angels in America, Les Blancs, Ma Rainey's Black Bottom, wonder.land (National); Passing Strange, The Homecoming, Mandela, Changing Destiny, Fairview, Death of a Salesman (& West End), The Convert. The Mountaintop, The Emperor (Young Vic); Two Strangers**

(Carry a Cake Across New York) (& West End); The Purists, Mlima's Tale, Retrograde, The Wife of Willesden, Pass Over, The Son (Kiln); Barcelona, Waiting for Godot, Long Days Journey Into Night, Opening Night, Enemy of the People, Ulster American, Sunset Boulevard, Best of Enemies, The Glass Menagerie, To Kill a Mockingbird, Cock, 2:22 A Ghost Story, Get Up Stand Up! The Bob Marley Musical, Constellations (& Donmar), Uncle Vanya, Tina - The Tina Turner Musical, Matilda, The Goat, or Who Is Sylvia, Dreamgirls (West End); The Human Body, Clyde's, A Doll's House Part II, Marys Seacole, Love and Other Acts of Violence, [BLANK] (Donmar); Rock 'n' Roll, Death of a Black Man, Caroline, or Change (& West End/Chichester Festival) (Hampstead); August in England, Leave Taking, F**k The Polar Bears (Bush); Newsies (Troubadour); Jitney, Misanthropes (Old Vic); Blue/Orange (& Oxford Playhouse/Theatre Royal Bath) White Noise, A Very Very Very Dark Matter (Bridge); Richard II (Globe); Death of a Salesman (Royal Exchange); Little Shop of Horrors, Peter Pan (Regents Park Open Air); Twilight LA, Eclipsed, The Rise & Shine of Comrade Fiasco (Gate).

Television includes: **Silo, The Baby, Mood, The Power, Small Axe.**

Film includes: **The Ministry of Ungentlemanly Warfare, Girl, Drift, Silent Twins, Midas Man, Silent Twins, Death on the Nile.**

Mimî M Khayisa (Bonolo)

Theatre includes: **Midsummer Mischief Festival, Cordelia, Hamlet (& US Tour), Wendy & Peter Pan, Taming of the Shrew (RSC); The Convert (Gate); Soul (Royal & Derngate/Hackney Empire); Sky Hawk (Theatr Clwyd).**

Television includes: **Mr Selfridge, Catherine Called Birdy, The Legend of Tarzan, The Witcher, Earthstorm, In The Long Run, Black Earth Rising, Rellik, Doctor Who, Yonderland.**

Film includes: **Catherine Called Birdy, Star Wars: Episode IX - The Rise of Skywalker, The Legend of Tarzan, Cinderella, Jack Ryan: Shadow Recruit.**

Sifiso Mazibuko (Sihle)

Theatre includes: **Ain't Too Proud (Prince Edward Theatre); Hamilton, Motown the Musical (West End); Dreamgirls The Musical (Teatro); Malindadzimu (Hampstead); I, Medea (SABAB Theatre); A Land Without People (Courtyard); The First Actress (Teatro Technis); Dancers (New York International Fringe Festival); The Tempest (Flute Theatre); The Theatre is a Blank page (The Wexner Centre for Arts).**

Television includes: **The Winter King, Willow, Similla's Sense of Snow, Masters of The Air.**

Film includes: **Here Be Giants, Pretville.**

Nancy Medina (Director)

Theatre includes: **Choir Boy (Bristol Old Vic); The Darkest Part of the Night (Kiln); Moreno (Theatre503); Trouble in Mind (National); Two Trains Running (Royal & Derngate/ETT); Strange Fruit (Bush); The Half God of Rainfall (Birmingham Rep/Kiln); Yellowman (Young Vic); Fefu and her Friends, Icarus, Pigeon English, Crimes of the Heart (Bristol School of Acting).**

Nancy is the Artistic Director of Bristol Old Vic and Co-Founder of Bristol School of Acting.

Martha Mamo (Stage Manager)

For the Royal Court: **The Pride, A Miracle.**

As stage manager theatre credits include: **Follow the Signs (Fuse); Ginger Johnson Blows Off, Realism, Mongrel Island (Soho); A Winters Tale, Women Beware Women (Globe); First Encounters Julius Caesar/ Comedy of Errors (RSC); Now and Then (English Theatre Frankfurt); The Painter, Light Shining Down On Buckinghamshire (Arcola); Way up Stream, Running Wild (Chichester); Kursk (Young Vic/Fuel/Sound and Fury).**

As prop supervisor theatre credits: **Doctor Faustus, Hamlet, the Alchemist, King Lear, The Tempest, Antony and Cleopatra (RSC); The Witches (National); Macbeth, Human Body (Donmar).**

Elena Peña (Sound Designer)

For the Royal Court: **The Legends of Them, Giant, Blue Mist, Baghdaddy, two Palestinians go dogging, seven methods of killing kylie jenner, Maryland, Living Newspaper.**

Other theatre includes: **A Tupperware of Ashes, The Hot Wing King, Trouble In Mind, Sweat, Nora: A Doll's House, Macbeth, Mountains, Rockets And Blue Lights Brainstorm (& Company3) (National); The Wedding Band (Lyric); Liberation Squares, The Memory of Water (Nottingham Playhouse); Cinderella (Brixton House); The Magic Finger (Unicorn); As You Like It (RSC); Wuthering Heights (China Plate/ UK Tour); Songs Across the Sueniverse (Sherman); Misty (Shed NYC); Silence (Donmar/Tara); The Chairs (Almeida); Seven Methods of Killing Kylie Jenner (Riksteatern, Sweden); The Darkest Part of The Night, Reasons You Shouldn't Love Me; Snowflake, The Kilburn Passion, Arabian Nights (Kiln); The Remains of the Day (Royal and Derngate); Autoreverse (BAC); Misty (& West End), Going Through, HIR, Islands (Bush); Thick As Thieves (Clean Break).**

Dance includes: **Patrias, Quimeras (Sadlers Wells/Paco Peña Flamenco Company).**

Television/online includes: **Have Your Circumstances Changed?, Brainstorm, The Astro Science Challenge.**

Radio includes: **Rockets & Blue Lights, The Meet Cute, Twelve Years, Duchamps Urinal.**

Installation includes: **Have Your Circumstances Changed?, Yes These Eyes Are The Windows (ArtAngel).**

Awards include: **Offie On Comm Award for Best Audio Production (Rockets & Blue Lights).**

Elena is an Associate Artist for Inspector Sands.

Emily Mei-Ling Pearce (Assistant Stage Manager)

Theatre credits include: **Slave Play (Nöel Coward); My Neighbour Totoro (Barbican); The Secret Life of Bees (Almeida); Only An Octave Apart (Wilton's Music Hall); Treason in Concert, Kinky Boots in Concert, Chess the Musical in Concert (Royal Drury Lane); Paradise Now! (Bush); Lotus Beauty (Hampstead); A Place for We (Park); and Pippin (Charing Cross).**

Robyn Rainsford (Jess)

Theatre includes: **Julius Caesar (Marylebone); Midsummer Nights Dream; Antony and Cleopatra (The Willow Globe); Macbeth (Theatr Clwyd); Black Bird (South African State Theatre); Hamlet (Johannesburg Civic Theatre); Strategy of Grey (Johannesburg Kingsway Theatre); Taming of the Shrew (Artscape Theatre); Othello, Annie (Natal Playhouse).**

Television includes: **Tali Babes, Here's to Good Times.**

Film includes: **Harvest, Broken Bird, Harry's Game, Love Life, Letters to April, Ballade Vir 'n Enkelling.**

Olivia Roberts
(Deputy Stage Manager)

For the Royal Court: **Living Newspaper, Queer Upstairs, Superhoe.**

Theatre includes: **Death of England: The Plays (Bill Kenwright/West End); The Other Boleyn Girl (Chichester Festival); Never Have I Ever (Chichester, Minerva); Spring Awakening (Almeida); The Ferryman (Sonia Friedman Productions/West End). Mosquitoes (National).**

Mark Simmonds
(Modelmaking & Drawing)

As assistant for the Royal Court : **Jerusalem, Wig Out! Choir Boy, The Winterling, Stoning Mary, Bone.**

Scott Sparrow (Christopher)

Theatre includes: **Madhouse, King Lear, Glengarry Glen Ross (& UK Tour), Strangers on a Train (West End); Wendy and Peter Pan (Leeds Playhouse); Clybourne Park (Woolly Mammoth); The Zoo Story, Buried Child, Mephisto, The Real Inspector Hound (The Mechanicals); Women Beware Women (Cockpit, Cape Town); A Lie of the Mind (University of Cape Town Little Theatre); Decadence (Old Mutual Theatre); Elizabeth (The Little Theatre).**

Film includes: **The Foreigner, Dredd, Safe House, London Has Fallen, Genius, Kidnap and Ransom, Critical, Strike Back, Death Race 2, The Runaway, Beaver Falls, Flight of the Storks, Wild at Heart.**

Scott is also a playwright and has written and produced three plays: **Performers' Travel Guide, Isabella and Dinner with the 42s.**

Tatenda Shamiso
(Associate Director)

As writer/performer for the Royal Court: **NO I.D.**

As associate director other theatres include: **For Black Boys Who Have Considered Suicide When the Hue Gets Too Heavy (West End); Choir Boy (Bristol Old Vic).**

As assistant director, other theatres include: **Wolves on Road (Bush); A Streetcar Named Desire (Almeida/ Phoenix); Bootycandy (Gate).**

As director other theatres include: **1884 (Shoreditch Town Hall); Housewarming (Theatre Peckham).**

As actor, other theatres include: **Sundown Kiki Reloaded (Young Vic).**

Awards include: **Evening Standard Theatre Award for Emerging Talent, Arts Foundation Futures Award for Theatre Writing.**

ULTZ (Designer)

For the Royal Court: **Jerusalem (& Broadway/West End), The River (& Broadway), Mojo (& West End), Torn, Choir Boy, Wig Out!, The Westbridge, Chicken Soup with Barley, Off the Endz, The Family Plays, The Winterling, Stoning Mary, A Girl in a Car with a Man, Fresh Kills, The Weather/Bear Hug, Bone, Fallout, The Night Heron, Fireface, Lift Off.**

Other theatre includes: **Skeleton Crew (Donmar); Play On! (Talawa); Death of England Trilogy (& West End), Ma Rainey's Black Bottom, Blood and Gifts, The Ramayana (National); La Musica, The Changeling, The Beauty Queen of Leenane (Young Vic); Iya-Ile, The Estate, The Gods Are Not To Blame (Tiata Fahodzi/Arcola/ Soho); Boy, Against, Richard II (Almeida); The Harder They Come (& Barbican/ West End); Pied Piper - a Hip Hop Dance Revolution (& Barbican), Da Boyz, Jean Genet's play The Blacks Remixed, The Public, Tambo and Bones, Kingston 14 (Stratford East).**

Opera includes: **La Clemenza di Tito, Gloriana (Royal Opera House); Lohengrin, The Rake's Progress, La Clemenza di Tito, Xerxes (Bavarian State Opera); Ariodante (Aix-en-Provence Festival/Dutch National Opera); Macbeth, Falstaff (Glyndebourne Festival); Cavalleria Rusticana/I Pagliacci, The Bitter Tears of Petra von Kant, Powder Her Face (ENO).**

Awards include: **Olivier Award for Best Set Design, Olivier Award for Outstanding Achievement in an Affiliate Theatre, Off West End Award for Best Set Design, UK Theatre Award, Best Designer for Tambo and Bones.**

THE ROYAL COURT THEATRE

The Royal Court Theatre is the writers' theatre. It is a leading force in world theatre for cultivating and supporting writers - undiscovered, emerging and established.

Since 1956, we have commissioned and produced hundreds of writers, from John Osborne to Mohamed-Zain Dada. Royal Court plays from every decade are now performed on stages and taught in classrooms and universities across the globe.

Through the writers, the Royal Court is at the forefront of creating restless, alert, provocative theatre about now. We open our doors to the unheard voices and free thinkers that, through their writing, change our way of seeing.

We strive to create an environment in which differing voices and opinions can co-exist. In current times, it is becoming increasingly difficult for writers to write what they want or need to write without fear, and we will do everything we can to rise above a narrowing of viewpoints.

Through all our work, we strive to inspire audiences and influence future writers with radical thinking and provocative discussion.

🐦 royalcourt 📘 royalcourttheatre

Supported using public funding by
**ARTS COUNCIL
ENGLAND**

Bristol Old Vic

Bristol Old Vic is the UK's longest continuously running theatre and has welcomed millions of people through its doors since opening nearly 260 years ago.

Led by Executive Director Charlotte Geeves and Artistic Director Nancy Medina, and with investment from Arts Council England, the organisation is committed to platforming and creating opportunities for the multitude of stories that Bristol and the UK have to offer.

Bristol Old Vic offers a year-round programme of inspiring, original new work – recently including the European Premiere of Matthew López's Reverberation, Nkenna Akunna's cheeky little brown with tiata fahodzi, and the new musical Starter for Ten. It also has one of UK theatre's biggest learning and engagement programmes; and has recently relaunched its artist development programme, including a five-year commitment to new writing which includes working with writer, Winsome Pinnock. Plus, through Bristol Old Vic On Screen, audiences across the world have seen its productions live or on demand.

"We will make a theatre which is for our whole community. Not a passive place, but one of activism. Not one voice, but many. We will ask questions of ourselves and of Bristol. We invite you to come on in and help us make this building sing with possibility."
– Nancy Medina, Artistic Director

bristololdvic.org.uk

Bristol Old Vic Staff

Artistic Director **Nancy Medina**
Executive Director **Charlotte Geeves**
Director of Producing and Programming **Jessica Campbell**
Producers **Giles Chiplin and Ruby Gilmour**
Assistant Producer **Charlotte Churm**
Literary Manager **Ben Atterbury**
Director of Production and Operations **Dave Harraway**
Production Manager **Aled Thomas**
Deputy Production Manager **Chloe Ashley**
Head of Marketing **Alice Wheeler**
Head of Communications **Amanda Adams**
Communications Officer **Parys Gardener**

Supported using public funding by Arts Council England

BRISTOL OLD VIC SUPPORTERS

We extend our thanks to the individuals and organisations that generously support Bristol Old Vic's work.

PRINCIPLE SUPPORT

 Supported using public funding by
ARTS COUNCIL ENGLAND

PROGRAMME SUPPORT

John Ellerman
Foundation

 Genesis
FOUNDATION

T   H   E
MACKINTOSH
FOUNDATION

 Quartet
Community
Foundation

BackstageTrust

Together with The 29th May 1961 Charitable Trust, Antonia Watson Foundation, The Garrick Charitable Trust and Wingate Foundation.

PROJECT SUPPORT

The Wolfson*
Foundation    Theatres Trust

CORPORATE SUPPORT

 VWV

With special thanks to Bristol Old Vic's individual supporters, Gold and Silver ticket holders and members.

Head of bristololdvic/support-us for a full list of our supporters and to find out about the many ways in which you can support our work.

ROYAL COURT SUPPORTERS

Our incredible community of supporters makes it possible for us to achieve our mission of nurturing and platforming writers at every stage of their careers. Our supporters are part of our essential fabric – they help to give us the freedom to take bigger and bolder risks in our work, develop and empower new voices, and create world-class theatre that challenges and disrupts the theatre ecology.

To all our supporters, thank you. You help us to write the future.

PUBLIC FUNDING

ARTS COUNCIL ENGLAND
Supported using public funding by

CHARITABLE PARTNERS

The Common Humanity Arts Trust

BackstageTrust

COCKAYNE

T. S. ELIOT FOUNDATION

JERWOOD
FOUNDATION

CORPORATE SPONSORS & SUPPORTERS
Aqua Financial Ltd
Cadogan
Concord Theatricals
Edwardian Hotels, London
NJA Ltd. – Core Values & Creative Management
Nick Hern Books
Prime Time
Sustainable Wine Solutions
Walpole

SIS
TER

CORPORATE MEMBERS
Bloomberg Philanthopies
Sloane Stanley

TRUSTS & FOUNDATIONS

Maria Björnson Memorial Fund
Martin Bowley Charitable Trust
Bruce Wake Charitable Trust
Chalk Cliff Trust
The Noël Coward Foundation
Cowley Charitable Foundation
The Davidson Play GC Bursary
The Fenton Arts Trust
Garrick Charitable Trust
The Golsoncott Foundation
The Lynne Gagliano Writers' Award
The Harold Hyam Wingate Foundation
John Lyon's Charity
The Marlow Trust
Clare McIntyre's Bursary
Old Possum's Practical Trust
Richard Radcliffe Charitable Trust
Rose Foundation
The Royal Borough of Kensington & Chelsea Arts Grant
Royal Victoria Hall Foundation
Theatres Trust
The Thistle Trust
The Thompson Family Charitable Trust

INDIVIDUAL SUPPORTERS

Artistic Director's Circle

Eric Abraham
Katie Bradford
Jeremy & Becky Broome
Clyde Cooper
Debbie De Girolamo &
Ben Babcock
Dominique & Neal Gandhi
Lydia & Manfred Gorvy
David & Jean Grier
Charles Holloway OBE
Linda Keenan
Andrew Rodger and Ariana
Neumann
Jack Thorne & Rachel Mason
Sandra Treagus for
ATA Assoc. LTD
Anonymous

Writers' Circle

Chris & Alison Cabot
Cas Donald
Robyn Durie
Ellie & Roger Guy
Melanie J. Johnson
Nicola Kerr
Héloïse and Duncan
Matthews KC
Emma O'Donoghue
Maureen & Tony Wheeler
Anonymous

Directors' Circle

Piers Butler
Fiona Clements
Professor John Collinge
Julian & Ana Garel-Jones
Carol Hall
Dr Timothy Hyde

Platinum Circle

Moira Andreae
Tyler Bollier
Katie Bullivant
Anthony Burton CBE
Matthew Dean
Emily Fletcher
Beverley Gee
Damien Hyland
Susanne Kapoor
David P Kaskel &
Christopher A Teano
Peter & Maria Kellner
Robert Ledger &
Sally Moulsdale
Frances Lynn
Mrs Janet Martin
Andrew McIver
Brian & Meredith Niles
Corinne Rooney
Anita Scott
Bhags Sharma
Dr Wendy Sigle
Rita Skinner
Brian Smith
Mrs Caroline Thomas
Ian, Victoria & Lucinda Watson
Sir Robert & Lady Wilson
Beverley Buckingham
The Edwin Fox Foundation
Lucy and Spencer De Grey
Madeleine Hodgkin
Barbara Minto
Timothy Prager
Sir Paul & Lady Ruddock
James and Victoria Tanner
Yannis Vasatis
Anonymous

With thanks to our Silver and Gold Supporters, and our Friends and Good Friends, whose support we greatly appreciate.

Let's be friends. With benefits.

Our Friends and Good Friends are part of the fabric of the Royal Court. They help us to create world-class theatre, and in return they receive early access to our shows and a range of exclusive benefits.

Join today and become a part of our community.

Become a Friend (from £40 a year)

Benefits include:

- Priority Booking
- Advanced access to £15 Monday tickets
- 10% Bar & Kitchen discount (including Court in the Square)

Become a Good Friend (from £95 a year)

In addition to the Friend benefits, our Good Friends also receive:

- Five complimentary playtexts for Royal Court productions
- An invitation for two to step behind the scenes of the Royal Court Theatre at a special event

Our Good Friends' membership also includes a voluntary donation. This extra support goes directly towards supporting our work and future, both on and off stage.

To become a Friend or a Good Friend, or to find out more about the different ways in which you can get involved, visit our website: royalcourttheatre. com/support-us

The English Stage Company at the Royal Court Theatre is a registered charity (No. 231242)

A GOOD HOUSE

Amy Jephta

'…and they loved their master more than their master loved himself.
They would give their life to save their master's house, quicker than the master would. If the master said,
"We got a good house here," the house Negro would say,
"Yeah, we got a good house here."'

Malcolm X, 'Message to the Grass Roots', 10 November 1963

'I remember that I'm invisible and walk softly so as not to awake the sleeping ones.
Sometimes it is best not to awaken them;
there are few things in the world as dangerous as sleepwalkers.'

Ralph Ellison, Invisible Man

4

Characters

SIHLE
BONOLO
ANDREW
JESS
LYNETTE
CHRIS

Setting

A cookie-cutter suburban home in the gated community of Stillwater.

Wherever that may be.

Time

Now.

Notations in the Text

Dialogue in (brackets) indicates line delivery sotto voce.

/ indicates the point of interruption for the following line.

Two-columned dialogue indicates simultaneous speech.

– at the beginning of a line indicates it continues uninterrupted from the previous break.

Italics indicates a drawn-out or prolonged/lingering delivery.

Bold indicates a hard emphasis or more definitive tone.

The Slinky Song

There are multiple versions of the Slinky song from various countries and time periods. In the performed version of the play, the lyrics of two adverts from the 1960s have been combined.

Verse 1 is from this ad: youtu.be/7acjValE1QI

Verse 2 is from this ad: youtu.be/ZAmJQkFSCp0

One Last Note

This text needs to go FAST. Like really fast. Don't give us time to catch our breath. All the chattering is really just to cover up the fact that the silence is oppressive.

And that no one is listening to anyone else. Not really.

So we almost don't breathe.

Until we do.

This text went to press before the end of rehearsals and so may differ slightly from the play as performed.

Prologue: Boyd Street

Darkness. The beep-beep of a truck reversing. Lights up on
SIHLE, *thirty-five, genteel and urbane.*

Waiting. Watching something happen over there. Hands on hips.
Ever patient.

CHRIS *in. Salt-of-the-earth type, forty-five, has somewhere to be.*
Not hostile, he approaches SIHLE.

CHRIS. Hey. Hey, buddy. Buddy!

SIHLE. Are you... hi. Is that me?

CHRIS. You didn't see me trying to get your attention just now?

SIHLE. You were? No, sorry I –

CHRIS. You didn't hear me hoot?

SIHLE. I heard *someone* hoot.

CHRIS. Didn't see me wave at you, flash my headlights?

SIHLE. Sorry.

CHRIS. Huh, okay, okay look, well I live here, I live over, over
    there at number fourteen. I'm tryna to get to work.
    And you've blocked the road with your uh – whatever *this*
    operation is.

SIHLE. Oh, the truck?

CHRIS. Your truck full of cement and concrete yes, that one.

SIHLE. The guys have gone to offload, shouldn't be too long.

CHRIS. Can you move it out the way though? I'm running late.

SIHLE. Fair enough. I'm sorry.

CHRIS. That's fine, but can you?

SIHLE. Well no, *I* can't. Not me personally.

CHRIS. Why the hell not?

SIHLE. Not my truck.

CHRIS. You said it was your truck.

SIHLE. Didn't say it was, no.

CHRIS. Then whose is it?

SIHLE. The guy who's gone to offload.

CHRIS. And who are you?

SIHLE. Sihle. Mbatha.

CHRIS. Sihle, okay, well – now who can move the bloody truck if not you, Sihle Mbatha?

SIHLE. The driver. I'm sure as soon as he's back –

CHRIS. Oh for fuckssakes what's the truck doing here this time of morning, man?

SIHLE. We're renovating.

CHRIS. Who's renovating.

SIHLE. *We are*.

CHRIS. You moving in here or something, what?

SIHLE. We just bought the place.

CHRIS (*surprised by that*). The Steins' old place?

SIHLE. I think so. I guess so, I don't know who the Steins are.

CHRIS. Nice people. I'm sure you are too, so, congrats. But you're gonna have to respect the neighbourhood rules, I don't think they're unreasonable. No blocking driveways, no idling, no hooting. No loud music, no parties, that sort of thing.

SIHLE. Not a fan of parties.

CHRIS. I mean a neighbourhood is worth nothing if we don't have some order, you know? Semblance of decency and respect.

SIHLE. I get it, Chris, thank you. And as soon as the guys are done inside they'll come back here, move the truck, we'll be out your hair.

CHRIS. Yeah no, fine. I don't want you to get the wrong impression or anything. We're very welcoming here in Stillwater. Very open.

SIHLE. I'm happy to hear that.

CHRIS. We've lived alongside one another for a long time and we've realised, you know, there's a, a way of coexisting. A way of living amongst friends and neighbours.

SIHLE. And what way is that?

CHRIS. Well. The way of Stillwater.

SIHLE. I'll have this moved for you.

CHRIS. I'd appreciate it, my man. You have a good day now.

CHRIS *walks off.*

SIHLE *stares after him. Intrigued.* SIHLE *takes his time leaving as –*

Scene One

Three moments unfold simultaneously:

Way back there in the shadows, behind some sort of screen, we see moving shapes coming together. Like a children's pop-up book or a marionette, something's rising up, assembling itself. Magic!

In a bit, the collection of shapes and shadows will start to resemble something.

It's a shack. A shanty house. A makeshift dwelling. Whatever you want to call it.

Four walls. Flat roof. A door. Distinctive.

In the foreground, BONOLO (*black, early thirties, sophisticated without trying too hard*) *enters. She looks at the empty space for a few beats.*

SIHLE *enters too.*

They roam around for a bit. Occasionally they catch each other's eye. They smile. Some secret language passes between them.

BONOLO. Ours?

SIHLE. Ours.

They roam some more.

And as this continues, the world begins to unfold around them.

Four figures slip in and begin to assemble, in the dim light, an entire living room – couches, armoires, a wet bar, etc. A beautifully decorated and furnished suburban frieze.

The four figures doing the creating are ANDREW,
LYNETTE, CHRIS *and* JESS.

They bring in and assemble this good, tasteful house while
BONOLO *and* SIHLE *look at everything, smile, share
glances. So many lovely things.*

Detailed.

On the coffee table, in the centre of the room, LYNETTE
*arranges a small spread. A cheese platter. Some fruit.
Modest but (no overstating this) in perfect taste.*

ANDREW *and* JESS *leave.*

LYNETTE *and* CHRIS *stay.*

Just waiting – and watching – as SIHLE *and* BONOLO
*explore their house. Their eyes track the couple as they pick
things up, put things down, run their hands over things.*

Then BONOLO *squeals, runs into* SIHLE*'s arms. He
embraces her, swings her around.*

BONOLO *has a moment where she's uninhibited. But then
she gathers herself – very subtly, not making a fuss over it –
and disengages from* SIHLE*'s embrace. She smiles.*

*She goes over to the wet bar. She takes some glasses off
a shelf. She turns on the tap. Water flows. She grins at*
SIHLE, *delighted.*

BONOLO. It works. Look, it works.

SIHLE. Very nice.

BONOLO *rinses red wine glasses.*

SIHLE *takes up an armchair across from* LYNETTE *and*
CHRIS *as the lights on the room start to fade up slowly,
slowly.*

They all wait for BONOLO *to finish.*

*Eventually we can pick out that an entire living room's been
assembled in here. And everything's gorgeous. An interior*

designer's wet dream. Touches of globally inspired Afro-chic.
Centre spread of ELLE Decoration. *Eclectic, but grown folk*
live here.

LYNETTE (*a subtly nip-and-tucked forty-five*) *looks over at*
BONOLO *occasionally, willing her to finish.* CHRIS
surreptitiously glances at his phone, fielding text messages.
SIHLE *just waits. The three occasionally share glances,*
small smiles.

Then they wait some more.

Oh, and that structure way back there? It's going to stay
there throughout the play. Slowly developing, growing,
morphing, sprouting. Weed-like.

Anyway, this whole thing has gone on for quite a while. So
we're kind of relieved when finally, FINALLY, BONOLO
brings over the four glasses she's been polishing, holding
them by the stem, the bottle of red in the other hand.

And as she sets these down the lights explode ON into –

Scene Two

BONOLO. There we go.

LYNETTE. Wow.

BONOLO. Right? I've learned –

LYNETTE. (Just wow, thank you.)

BONOLO. – that everything goes down better with a ripe
cheese plate and a vintage Merlot.

SIHLE. Looks beautiful darling.

CHRIS. My kinda girl this.

LYNETTE. Well if no one's going to dig in then I will.

SIHLE. Help yourself.

LYNETTE. Can I pour anyone a glass / of

BONOLO. **Oh wait!** *Waaait*, hang on! Hold on hold on.

> LYNETTE *freezes, bottle in hand.* BONOLO *hastens back to the kitchen. Roots around, comes up with a wine aerator, brings it to the group. Takes the bottle from* LYNETTE.

CHRIS. What's – ?

SIHLE. Aerator.

BONOLO. Aerator. For the wine it… aerates.

LYNETTE. That is *fancy*.

SIHLE. It lets the wine breathe.

CHRIS. Breathe? How's that hey, I didn't know wine needed to / breathe.

BONOLO. It can, it does, it's
a living thing. Sihle took
me on this tour of Sardegna
on our fourth –   SIHLE. Third, I think.

BONOLO. Third! Anniversary. This is how they drink it in Italy. We got this aerator in Italy. Wine is an organism they said, it evolves (and who are we to argue), it grows, it ripens –

SIHLE. It dies, eventually.

LYNETTE. I've never been.

SIHLE. Dead?

LYNETTE. To Italy.

CHRIS. We visit Lyn's sister in Swindon once a year, that's as close as we get.

BONOLO. To Italy?

CHRIS. No, to death.

BONOLO. Oh you guys *must*
    go to Sardinia. There's this
    darling little village in
    Barigadu, no one knows
    about this place –   LYNETTE. I would love –

BONOLO. – they call it Sorradile, you **would** love it. The
    landscape, these vistas, these *people* are so pure, just pure,
    salt of the earth, connected to… and the wine! The wine.

CHRIS. *Ahh*, Sardinia, we
    will, we should, uh Lyn–
                                          LYNETTE. We absolutely
                                          will.

BONOLO. You *muuuust*, Italy can have me any day.

LYNETTE. You two are so chic! So… *global*.

    Everyone goes quiet again as they watch BONOLO *glug the*
    wine into glasses. She holds the glass at the correct angle too.

    CHRIS*'s phone beeps. He checks his messages while they*
    wait (he'll do this throughout, splitting his attention between
    the phone and the conversation, but trying very hard not to
    let his distraction show).

    Four glasses. That takes a while. BONOLO *hands a glass to*
    each of them.

SIHLE. Well. Neighbours. Welcome to our house.

CHRIS. And what a house.

    They clink their glasses, take a sip. 'HMM's and 'AAH's all
    around.

    And what wine!

LYNETTE. So good. And these interiors, I love what you've
    done with the place. *Eclectic.*

BONOLO. Oh, *pff.*

LYNETTE. Now did you get someone in or / did you

BONOLO. Oh no-no-no, I've always had an eye.

CHRIS. The, uh, layout is quite different to ours, hey Lyn?
Floor plans, I'm talking about.

LYNETTE. I mean these houses are all generally the same but
that's what makes them wonderful, right, they're a starting
point for your imagination. A blank canvas if you will.

CHRIS. (Look at her now, trying to sell you a house you
already own.)

LYNETTE. No Chris, I'm just saying. We kept our layout the
same doesn't mean it's the only way to imagine the space.
Look at what Bonolo's managed to do here.

BONOLO. We had some renovations done.

CHRIS. Right, of course you did, I forget, that was when you
had all the guys in with the trucks and the –

SIHLE. *Ah* yeah, sorry about all that.

CHRIS. No it wasn't at all –

SIHLE. I still feel bad about the uh / that's how we met isn't it?

CHRIS. – an issue, years ago now. Small little thing. / Tiny.

LYNETTE. What thing is that?

CHRIS. Nothing. Nothing, nothing.

SIHLE. It was how I first met Chris. Years ago.

CHRIS. Two years ago, yeah.

SIHLE. That's before we even knew one other.

CHRIS. Way before.

LYNETTE. What happened? I've never heard this story.

CHRIS. It was silly. I'm trying to reverse out and / and

SIHLE. And our guys – the builders – they've blocked the road.
Just parked their truck right in the middle of the street. Chris's
trying to get to work, he's in a hurry, I have the builders up my
ass that day and anyway, you know how it goes –

LYNETTE. Oh *I* see how it goes.

CHRIS. That was before I knew you, though.

SIHLE. We'd just moved in, barely a week.

CHRIS. I was rushed off my feet that day.

LYNETTE. As he is every day, (I'm always telling him to slow down / to meditate).

BONOLO. (*Hmmm*, one must.)

SIHLE. Well it was all fine in the end. That was, like you said, before –

CHRIS. Before we got to know / you.

SIHLE. Right.

LYNETTE. Even ten minutes a day they say of meditation does wonders.

BONOLO (*bored of this story*). So yes, I have an eye. I decorated it, chose the fittings, did the soft furnishings. This rug is from a souk in the Medina quarter.

Off LYNETTE*'s blank stare.*

Marrakesh.

LYNETTE. Is that where you're from, you have, uh, ties to Marrakesh or –

BONOLO. None at all. I'll show you the bedroom later, the headboard was a custom – you'll die.

CHRIS. I am *so* glad we're finally doing this. It's long overdue.

SIHLE. It really is.

BONOLO. Exactly what *I* said.

CHRIS. I've been saying to
Lynette. We live right next
to the Mbathas. We see
them mornings, afternoons,
say hello we (didn't I say
this Lyn?), all in passing,
but we never *connect*.   LYNETTE. Did, yes.

LYNETTE. I can't believe I've never been in this house.

SIHLE. Not once.

LYNETTE. Life gets so busy, you know, the old hamster wheel, we're always on to the next thing. We churn / we churn

BONOLO. I know / *I know.*

LYNETTE. And we *lose* each other in the process. To sometimes take a moment and connect is, it's, what's the word, it's valuable.

SIHLE. Vital.

CHRIS. Important.

BONOLO. And here we are! Doing the connecting.

A breath. <u>Finally</u>.

SIHLE. Try the cheese.

LYNETTE. Oh I'll volunteer, (this looks very good).

BONOLO. (Do the Brie first, use the knife / there's a system here.)

LYNETTE. (You'll have to guide me through it, I don't want to mess up the order.)

CHRIS. So Sihle, remind me again, you're in...?

SIHLE. Securities.

CHRIS. Oh, that's right. And which security company is that?

LYNETTE. No love, securi*ties*.

CHRIS. Oh riiiiiiight, right of course. The, the um, the financial guys, the brokers and so on, the Forex traders.

SIHLE. I'm not a Forex trader, no. It's a mid-sized firm. We have offices in Sandton and in Canary Wharf and we –

LYNETTE. Wow, this Brie is *ripe*. Where did you –

CHRIS. Darling you've interrupted Sihle, you were saying?

LYNETTE. (Sorry.)

SIHLE. No it's not that interesting, when you're outside the financial world it's really not / that interesting at all.

CHRIS. Try me.

BONOLO. Don't get him started, Chris!

CHRIS. No, try me.

SIHLE. Okay. So – my job involves monitoring instrument valuation, uh, analysing security valuation exceptions, recently I've been pulled into equity valuations, ratio analysis –

BONOLO. Nobody knows what you're talking about.

CHRIS. Well no, that all sounds *very* intriguing.

BONOLO. He's very smart. You're very smart, aren't you?

SIHLE. So they say.

BONOLO. So his bosses say. They've just made Sihle partner.

LYNETTE. Incredible!

SIHLE. It's been a long time coming, (thank you Lynette).

BONOLO. Well after nine years to be –

CHRIS. (Well done.)

SIHLE. (Thank you.)

BONOLO. – first black senior manager, first black partner, after nine years, I mean, can you imagine, to still be the first black *any*thing?

LYNETTE. Excellent. It's time. It's your time.

BONOLO. Is what I'm saying, it's *been* his time. There are partners who came in *after* him –

SIHLE. Let's not get into all that now, the point is. Tonight we celebrate.

CHRIS. You heard today?

SIHLE. Yesterday afternoon. We haven't had time to plan /
a dinner or –

LYNETTE. Oh no, are we imposing on your celebrations?

SIHLE. Not at all, this isn't it.

LYNETTE. I'm sorry if we're –

BONOLO. It's fine Lynette, we'll have a little soirée soon, for
now we're just happy you're here.

CHRIS. Well now we *are* here, let's have a toast to Sihle. On
your promotion. About bloody time.

They clink glasses. Clinkclinkclinkclink.

LYNETTE. I think it's just great that companies are more aware
of transformation, it's encouraging.

BONOLO. They don't have a choice.

CHRIS. No they don't really have a choice, do they? I mean not
in this climate.

LYNETTE. Which is a good thing.

CHRIS. *Ex*-cellent thing.

LYNETTE. People like Sihle must be rewarded for their hard
work.

BONOLO. Which climate is that?

CHRIS. Hm?

BONOLO. When you said 'this climate', which climate were
you –

LYNETTE. Oh I think Chris means the, um – what do you
mean? / (Sorry love, the wine is already going to my head –
such good wine.)

BONOLO. (Let me top that up.)

CHRIS. Well we're talking about affirmative action aren't we?
The black empowerment policies and such. Impossible to do
business these days if you don't have the status of –

LYNETTE. As it should be.

BONOLO. S*uuu*re, but that's not the reason Sihle got the job.

CHRIS. No. *No*. I'm just saying context is certainly a *factor* in –

BONOLO. The context is nine years of hard graft.

LYNETTE. Right.

BONOLO. Nine years of a salary barely adjusted for inflation, an increase in workload, he would get home some nights at nine, ten p.m., barely able to sleep for the noise in his head, this constant noise.

SIHLE. I knew it would be a long road.

LYNETTE. That's loyalty.

BONOLO. And in return for loyalty he got nothing. For nine years.

CHRIS. I don't doubt you proved yourself, Sihle, not for a second.

SIHLE. Thank you Chris.

CHRIS. I mean there are cases where the… one of the guys who's on the WhatsApp group, David. You know David.

SIHLE. I don't think we do.

BONOLO. (Which WhatsApp group?)

CHRIS. He's over on Birch Street. (Nothing interesting, just a coupla old friends shooting shit.)

LYNETTE. (CHRIS.)

CHRIS. (Sorry.)

LYNETTE. David Jansen. His wife is Elena?

SIHLE. Don't think we know them, no.

CHRIS. In any case. David's in construction, started with kitchen installations. From the ground up mind you, invested his own money with a bit of a bank loan, poured it into this

business. Expands to bigger contracts, bigger clients,
corporates, he did corporate offices and such. Expands into
renovation, into buildings.

And eventually (this is now four years later) eventually he
wants to go after bigger jobs, you see. Government tenders
and so on. He's told he can't bid. Certification's not in order.
So now for David there's this ceiling he can't get past.
A literal ceiling to how far he can expand his business, this
business he built with his own hands. Because, well, you
know. He's white.

BONOLO. Is he? Pity.

CHRIS. Exactly. Exactly. *That's* the great shame.

LYNETTE. No well not *the* great shame. *A* shame, maybe, one
of many. But not in Sihle's case.

CHRIS. No not at all. You, of course, are an excellent asset.

BONOLO (*in very good humour*). How do you know?

CHRIS. Come again?

BONOLO. How do you know he's an excellent asset?

CHRIS. Well, that's what – I know he is, you said how hard he
works, the hours, how smart...

BONOLO. He's an excellent asset because you know him?

CHRIS. I don't understand the question?

BONOLO. That wasn't a question, never mind.

LYNETTE. I don't understand either but, I'd like to?

BONOLO. No it's just Chris's saying Sihle deserved the
promotion, of course **he** deserved it, because Chris knows him.

SIHLE. I think that's what Chris is saying, yes.

CHRIS. Yes, from my knowledge of him –

BONOLO. So in his case all's good and fair.

CHRIS. Right.

SIHLE. Right. Okay, good. Settled.

Leave it there. For just a few seconds before –

BONOLO. Whereas if you *didn't* know him you would think –

CHRIS. Okay, hold on, there's no way of you knowing *what* I'd think. There's no way of *me* knowing what I'd think, if I didn't know him.

BONOLO. You said you had a different thought about him, that you thought differently before you knew him, that day in the driveway. But then he, uh, he changed your mind about him somehow, so… what were you thinking about him (I'm just curious) before he changed your mind, when your mind was still made up about him? Before.

LYNETTE. What – now – I'm very confused.

CHRIS. I think my brain's
been twisted into a few
knots I can't quite –

BONOLO. I'm not making
sense, forget it, sorry
I asked, just curious.

SIHLE. Can we move on now? This really isn't the best –

LYNETTE. *I agree.*

SIHLE. – use of our time. I mean there's always going to be something to disagree on in this climate.

LYNETTE. In all climates, precisely.

CHRIS. Disagreement's good, it's necessary. This country could do with more disagreement.

SIHLE. Oh no I don't think this country needs *more* disagreement.

CHRIS. No, that's right, I meant civil disagreement.

SIHLE. Civil, perhaps.

A beat while everyone dips around for the next thing. Maybe eats something.

CHRIS. So you two must know Andrew and Jess Fraser.

BONOLO. The new people?

CHRIS. I wouldn't say *new* –

BONOLO. Relatively new. In comparison to us.

LYNETTE. Yes in comparison to us who've lived here / for years.

CHRIS. Then of course, yes, relatively new. You must know them?

SIHLE. Don't think we do. I'm starting to think we don't know anyone.

CHRIS. They're around your age I think, youngsters.

BONOLO. (Ha, thanks for that.)

LYNETTE. Thirty-something, very nice people. I sold them their house. Number eight.

SIHLE. We haven't had the pleasure.

LYNETTE. You should take a walk down the cul-de-sac some time, just knock on the – I'm sure they'd love to meet you, they're so welcoming, *so* nice.

BONOLO. Why'd you ask?

CHRIS. About…? Oh no reason. Just thought you'd have met. They've been here about two months, s'that right, Lyn? Andrew manages a restaurant. Jess teaches yoga from their house.

SIHLE. *Oh* okay.

CHRIS. Andrew and Jess have a bit of a thing. Really small thing. And their small thing got us thinking.

BONOLO. A thing?

LYNETTE. Oh Chris love, we don't need to get into this right now, do we?

CHRIS. Well I don't mean to upset anyone.

SIHLE. What's upsetting?

LYNETTE. It's not upsetting, it's just inappropriate… for now.

BONOLO. Now I'm curious. Now you have to tell us what –

CHRIS. Well there's this *structure*…

LYNETTE. Chris…

CHRIS. No, you're right Lyn, let me call it what it is. Let me not say structure when I mean shack. I mean shack.

SIHLE. What shack, where?

CHRIS. That's the thing. It came out of nowhere. Sprang up from the dust.

LYNETTE. Well no – it couldn't've – someone put it there. Clearly, someone put it there.

BONOLO. Who?

CHRIS. Is the question. This is what we Do Not Know.

SIHLE. We haven't seen it, have we?

BONOLO. I don't think so.

LYNETTE. Just look out there right now. You can't miss the thing, it's an eyesore. Look.

SIHLE *gets up and goes to look out. He cranes a bit.*

SIHLE. Don't see anything.

LYNETTE. See the house far left in the cul-de-sac? That's Jess and Andrew, the face-brick house, number eight. And just across from the boot (that's called the boot), there's that empty plot of land and –

SIHLE. I see the plot…

LYNETTE. – if you lean to the left and sort of, you know what, maybe you can't see it from this angle.

SIHLE. I see the plot.

CHRIS. We've tried to find out who owns that plot but no answers.

LYNETTE. For now it's really just an empty piece of – overgrown grass, weeds, whoever was planning to build there dropped off some concrete blocks –

CHRIS. Bricks. Years ago now.

LYNETTE. What I'm saying is – the plot was empty. I'd been trying to get it on my books for ages, chasing dead ends with the municipality. See it's hidden enough that you can't really spot it from the road, unless you're *looking*. But it's not ideal to have this open piece of – rats, snakes / who knows what kind of wildlife –

BONOLO. (Do we have snakes in the suburbs?)

CHRIS. Which, we speculate, they were. The newcomers.

SIHLE. Snakes?

LYNETTE. *Looking*. For a piece of land.

SIHLE. *Ah*.

BONOLO. And you're saying this structure –

CHRIS. The shack.

BONOLO. – has people living there?

LYNETTE. Jess and Andrew couldn't tell. They haven't seen anyone come and go just yet. They suspect the ones who put it up have been operating 'under the radar'.

CHRIS. So to speak.

LYNETTE. Under the radar, coming and going at night, in the dark, that sort of thing.

SIHLE. Doing what, do you think?

CHRIS. This isn't what *we* think, let's just be clear –

LYNETTE. No, definitely not what we –

CHRIS. – let's just be clear about that. But Andrew speculates they could just be, you know. Living there. Perhaps making plans.

BONOLO. *Uh-huh.* What kind of plans?

LYNETTE. To stay. To relocate. Here. To Stillwater.

BONOLO. But Jess and Andrew have not physically *seen* any *people*.

CHRIS. Not yet. Which is a feat because, as you know, Jess works from home.

SIHLE. Teaches yoga, right.

CHRIS. Right. Her studio faces the front window, she's at that window all day. So at first the Frasers thought it was a joke, that eventually they'd come across someone living there, politely ask them about it. But now it's been, what, ten days, no one's been seen and the shack is still there. So. What do you make of that?

Hmmm.

SIHLE. It's not ideal.

LYNETTE. I am *so* relieved to hear you say that, Sihle.

SIHLE. If it's true that people are living there it's not ideal at all.

LYNETTE. So relieved – thought it was just us who found it strange.

SIHLE. Well we live here too so.

CHRIS. Right. See, Lyn? I told you. They'd get it.

SIHLE. We get it!

CHRIS. Lyn didn't want to broach the subject because of… we know it can come across as a bit – I mean when you hear about what happened in the nextneighbourhoodover…

BONOLO. What happened *where*?

CHRIS. In the nextneighbourhoodover. So Lyn was worried it would be asking too much.

BONOLO. What would?

CHRIS. Well this thing got us thinking (god, this is the whole point of the story finally), it got us thinking that some other communities of our size have had great success with monitoring groups.

BONOLO. Monitoring groups, like an association?

LYNETTE. A rate-payers' association.

SIHLE. Like a Neighbourhood Watch.

CHRIS. We*lll* Neighbourhood Watches these days have unsavoury connotations, we don't mean to be *militant* about it. It would be more of a hybrid… y'know.

LYNETTE. Where rate-payers' associations are concerned with the culture and the living standards of an area, a Neighbourhood Watch is a more practical – patrols and such. But the Concerned Residents Group would serve both ends of that spectrum.

SIHLE. Not against the idea, if it made us all feel safer, bit more secure…

CHRIS. It would, it would give us some kind of formal structure, understand. A collective power. Because if we're going to take action here and uhm, clear out this plot, we'd need the community behind us. It can't just be something the Frasers want, or something **we** want, we'd all need to stand together, you see?

SIHLE. I see.

CHRIS. We'd need to approach the matter of the eviction in a way that's fair, reasonable. Doesn't create unnecessary –

SIHLE. *Right*.

CHRIS. – tension or stir up the media or (god forbid), the activists.

LYNETTE. We're not trying to make the front page here. We don't want to trend on social media. What's that term they use? *Drag* us, we don't want to be *dragged*.

CHRIS. So we'd need your help on this.

SIHLE. Yes, no, we support you one hundred per cent.

LYNETTE. This is *great*. Thank you for agreeing.

BONOLO. Agreeing to what?

CHRIS. To serving the eviction order. On behalf of the community.

SIHLE. Going the formal route is an excellent idea. And this community is our home, we love it here.

BONOLO. Who's serving the eviction order?

LYNETTE. You.

CHRIS. No – Lyn – *we,* you're the signatories, that's all, 'go ye forth!' kind of thing, the rest of us are right behind you.

BONOLO. You want **us** to knock on the shack's door, I don't…?

SIHLE. I mean the reason we bought into this community was for the sense of, you know, family. The safety aspect.

LYNETTE. And Stillwater's always been very safe. Historically.

BONOLO. And now it's not.

CHRIS. No, it's always been, it was, it is. It's not my intention to cause panic.

BONOLO. So then why – (sorry if I didn't, there's a lot coming at us here) –

LYNETTE. (Right at you, of course.)

BONOLO. – why do we also need this monitoring group?

CHRIS. It's a pre-emptive strike.

BONOLO. Because of the shack.

CHRIS. Not *because* – see it started like this, in the nextneighbourhoodover.

BONOLO. I'm just wondering how the arrival of these as-yet-unseen visitors, how that affects our safety? Should I be afraid?

CHRIS. Don't worry, we're not saying that, at least not yet. We're just not sure what the intentions are.

BONOLO. The intentions of the shack.

CHRIS. Of the people who put the shack there.

BONOLO. The invisible people.

CHRIS. We don't know who they are yet, *truuue*, but –

BONOLO. They may not even exist. If you've never seen them, if the shack came up out of nowhere, sprang up from the dust –

CHRIS. I didn't mean the *literal* / dust.

SIHLE. No *I* get you, I get what you're –

CHRIS. (You get it), it may be nothing and no one but it may also be the first of many.

BONOLO. A land-grab?

LYNETTE. Whoa, I don't think we need to be throwing around words like that – do you? – words like invasion or god forbid –

– right, and before you know it –

CHRIS. You know, all we're saying is it happens very quickly, literally overnight / and –

SIHLE. Kumele kube nzima njalo, neh? [*It must always be difficult, huh?*]

BONOLO. What?

Ungenzi kube nzima,
Bonolo. [*Don't make it
difficult, Bonolo.*]

LYNETTE. I'm sorry we...

SIHLE. Apologies.

CHRIS. Our Zulu isn't up to scratch, I'm afraid.

BONOLO. Neither is mine.

SIHLE. (Sorry about that, I –)

BONOLO. Who owns this piece of land?

CHRIS. Owns?

SIHLE. I thought Chris said –

BONOLO. Simply, whose piece of land is it?

LYNETTE. Like Chris said, we don't know.

BONOLO. You don't.

CHRIS. I've called the municipality, Lyn's logged a request for
the deeds papers, it appears this particular plot is sort of,
unaccounted for. A no-man's-land.

SIHLE. *Hm*. No man?

CHRIS. None at all.

SIHLE. So strange.

BONOLO. So it's nobody's.

CHRIS. Not officially, not until the municipality comes back
with the – (is she upset?)

SIHLE. Not at all.

BONOLO. Me? Not at all.

CHRIS. Okay, good.

BONOLO. Just getting it all straight in my head. We are forming an organisation –

CHRIS. Association.

BONOLO. – association, for the purpose of evicting one group of – and we don't even know if it *is* a group, it could be an individual – of squatters, from a piece of land none of us own.

CHRIS. I wasn't very clear, I'm sorry – we begin with the squatters, of course. The eviction order is only our first duty, a tiny thing, then we'd move on to other community concerns. The association has a larger purpose.

LYNETTE. Such as…

CHRIS. Holding the council accountable for the collection of trash, keeping an eye on climbing property rates, developments in the area, your traditional watchdog functions, et cetera, et cetera.

SIHLE. (Which I'd gladly volunteer my time to.)

CHRIS. And we'd love to have you.

SIHLE. I'd be happy to give my time to such an…

BONOLO *picks through her words very carefully.*

BONOLO. Doesn't it feel somewhat… that we're (sorry, is it just me?) ganging up against a few desperate human beings to evict them from an unoccupied piece of land in a cul-de-sac?

CHRIS. No one's ganging up, there's a… there's nothing *rogue* about our –

LYNETTE. Invisible human beings.

BONOLO. Come again?

LYNETTE. Invisible human beings, not desperate, you said it yourself just now, we don't know, we don't know who the people are, how many people there are, by saying *desperate* you're giving emotive qualities to people whose existence

you doubted mere minutes ago, you just said they didn't
exist, so how can they *also* be desperate?

CHRIS. (Lyn.)

LYNETTE. Am I not making sense?

SIHLE. No you're making perfect –

CHRIS. Let's maybe talk about this another time. I can see we
have some uh, it deserves some debate. It deserves cool
heads.

SIHLE. I'm cool.

BONOLO. Well everyone's not you, so.

Silence. BONOLO *begins to clear the glasses, plates, the
remainder of the cheeseboard. Everyone else watches
awkwardly for a few beats before* LYNETTE *jumps up and
begins to help.* BONOLO *lets* LYNETTE *get on with it as
she straightens up.*

My family, Lynette, as you asked, is from Cape Town. Most
of them live in a township called Langa. My mother grew up
twelve people to a rented council flat. My cousin,
Nomfundo, lives eight people and two babies to a one-
bedroom shanty with a tin roof. I am the first person in my
family to own the house I live in.

Beat.

LYNETTE. Do you want these in the kitchen?

BONOLO. Please.

LYNETTE *follows* BONOLO *to the kitchen.*

This whole time, CHRIS *has been thinking* –

CHRIS. If you met the Frasers...

LYNETTE. Chris, just / (drop it).

CHRIS. No I really think if they met the Frasers. Went to see
the structure –

SIHLE. The shack.

CHRIS. The shack, for yourselves. Give you an idea of what we're dealing with.

SIHLE. Sure. Sure.

CHRIS. Help you understand why it's so important to us, find a meeting point. Or hell, tell us if we're overreacting. I'm completely willing to accept that we may be.

SIHLE. That's generous, Chris.

CHRIS. If I've been insistent I really do apologise.

LYNETTE *and* BONOLO *re-enter from the kitchen.*

LYNETTE. We.

CHRIS. *We* really do apologise. I didn't mean to upset you, or make this wonderful evening uncomfortable. It's a tricky subject, I see that now. It's sensitive –

LYNETTE. (Like I said.)

CHRIS. – Like Lyn said, there are sensitivities here. I know what we must sound like. Paranoid, hysterical, actually, about a few sheets of metal. You know, it always starts with a few sheets of metal, but maybe that's all it is, on the face of it. Just a few sheets... of metal.

BONOLO. What it *is*...

During the following bit, LYNETTE *and* CHRIS *stay on the stage, but the lights start to close in* SIHLE *and* BONOLO *until it's just them two, staring each other down, circling each other, outside of time.*

LYNETTE *and* CHRIS *listen and watch from the darkness.*

What it is...
Is they're *threatened* by a *house*.

SIHLE. It's not a house.

BONOLO. *Hayi wena*, it's a structure with four walls and a roof, built for the purpose of living in.

SIHLE. There's no one living there.

BONOLO. They're threatened by what the house implies about the people who live there, by who those people may be.

SIHLE. And who may those people be?

BONOLO. **Black people.**

SIHLE. No one said anything about black people.

BONOLO. It was implied.

SIHLE. How do you *imply* black?

BONOLO. By the insistence that there are insiders and outsiders. And we sit here deciding that those people, in the shack, are outsiders.

SIHLE. And who are *we*?

BONOLO. We're the insiders, it appears.

SIHLE. But we're *black*.

BONOLO. Exactly. But, they say, we're not *that* kind of black.

SIHLE. Because we pay our home loan on time. Because we saved since we're eighteen so we could buy a property, legally. Because we went to university, educated ourselves, worked our asses off, do you remember the *sacrifices* we made?

BONOLO. So we're different.

SIHLE. Hell yes. *Hell yes*.

BONOLO. And whoever's living in that shack didn't go to school, doesn't work hard, doesn't possess intellect / doesn't –

SIHLE. Their supposed blackness can't mean we have anything in common. They may not even *be* black, you're defending four pieces of tin and a roof out of some righteous *crusade* of –

BONOLO. That shack could've been ours, if we were different people.

SIHLE. No. Your existence is finite. The possibilities for who you could've been is not an endless ream of. The margin isn't as narrow as you'd like to think. It's not luck, we're a world away from them. Look at *your* world. At this… cheese knife. At this fucking aerator. *This* is *you*.

BONOLO. I'm an aerator?

SIHLE. You are *this*, yes, this solid object, and that chair you're sitting on and that glass you're holding and *you are* –

BONOLO. And you're so sure of that, you're so sure these objects give me a solid state, that in possessing these solid things I am *seen*, that they *see me*, that we do exist, in the real world, that we're part of the noise and solidity of the things they perceive as real, our existence as rooted as our things are, that this house and its walls and all its nice objects *is what we are*, to them, under the skin.

SIHLE. Yes. Because this shit's made of brick, and we built it.

Lights snap change. We're back to –

BONOLO. What it *is*…

SIHLE. Is something to think about. And think we will.

CHRIS. Well look, we'll be out of your hair. Thank you for this.

LYNETTE. We really should be getting on, yes.

BONOLO. Thanks for popping by.

CHRIS. And really, what a pleasure, this was long overdue.

SIHLE. All ours.

CHRIS. I won't forget this wine in a hurry.

SIHLE. I'll send you the label, you should get some.

CHRIS. (I'll tear up the bottle   LYNETTE. Toodles, you two.
store if I have to.)

ALL (*ad lib*). Bye-bye. / Goodnight. / Sleep well! / We should do this again. / So lovely, this *house*. / Thanks-thanks-thanks. /

Safe home now. / Don't let the snakes get you! / Oh, ha-ha-ha.
(*Etc.*)

LYNETTE *and* CHRIS *exit.*

SIHLE *exhales. He's amused, baffled.*

Scene Three

BONOLO *starts to clean up. Slippers on, face off.* SIHLE
helps. They do that in silence for a beat or two.

BONOLO. They ate most of our cheese platter.

SIHLE. You asked them to.

BONOLO. I don't do half-ass hostess jobs. This is a Wüsthof
cheese knife, it's artisan, I've been saving it for an occasion.

SIHLE. This was an occasion.

BONOLO. I could've saved it for longer is what I mean.

He picks up the cheese knife. She takes it from him.

Use your hands.

SIHLE. Why do I have to –

BONOLO. Because the Wüsthof's for guests. It goes in the box,
the box goes in the cupboard.

SIHLE. Let me put the plastic back on the settee while we're at it.

BONOLO. Mock, but good impressions matter.

SIHLE. No, you're right, they were impressed.

BONOLO. And I think it was a smart call, on my part, to make
them feel at ease. You can't trust anyone these days,
especially neighbours. They could kill us in our sleep.

SIHLE. Luckily you don't sleep.

BONOLO. Doesn't hurt to be diplomatic.

SIHLE. *That* was you being diplomatic?

BONOLO. I gave it my best.

SIHLE. But with an agenda.

BONOLO. Somewhat.

SIHLE. So lying.

BONOLO. I was taking a leaf out your book. You lie.

SIHLE. No. In what context?

BONOLO. You say you're fine when you're not, you say you understand a point of view when you don't, I was playing the game as you play it. You say I get combative, I was trying a different approach.

SIHLE. It still felt combative.

BONOLO. I'm not that good at 'roll over and play dead', and what was this shit with the –

SIHLE. I want people to feel comfortable around me.

BONOLO. Yes no, sure. My opinion: sometimes you're soft.

SIHLE. Ayo no / come –

BONOLO. You let people off easy, you don't ask difficult questions. You don't want to… appear unlikeable. Especially to certain – don't kill me for this – especially to certain kinds of people.

SIHLE. I can tell by your face you have a specific example, (how did this become about me?)

BONOLO. (You made it about you), I do have a specific example.

SIHLE. By certain kinds of people you mean white people?

BONOLO. I **do** have a specific example.

SIHLE. I'm listening.

BONOLO. Remember we were at that drinks thing for Jackson-Briggs, you'd been there, like, a year or something? It was the first thing they invited us to.

SIHLE. Yes I remember, (have you told me this?)

BONOLO. (I haven't told you this.) And your colleagues kept calling you Slinky. They kept referring to you as Slinky this, Slinky that.

SIHLE. *Right.*

BONOLO. And I didn't understand it. You're skinny, I thought maybe that was – anyway. Slinky's not much easier to pronounce than Sihle so I didn't think that was it.

SIHLE. I don't know why either.

BONOLO. Is what you kept saying, right. And eventually, night went on, we were having a good laugh, you were talking to your boss, I was circling and ended up talking to that one guy, Lipman –

SIHLE. –schitz.

BONOLO. Shit what?

SIHLE. Lipschitz.

BONOLO. Lipschitz, right. Smarmy fucker.

SIHLE. He was the one who started with the nickname.

BONOLO. Cornered him at the bar, I ask him, why does everyone call my husband Slinky?

SIHLE. Don't tell me you got an answer.

BONOLO. I got an answer.

SIHLE. You knew this whole time?

BONOLO. Yep.

SIHLE. And? (Why haven't you told me this), and?

BONOLO. Well a Slinky is that child's toy, don't you know it? It appears to walk downstairs by itself. It makes a slinkety sound. Slinkslinkslink. There was that jingle, you know it.

SIHLE*'s drawing a blank.*

Everyone knows it.

BONOLO *sings the Slinky jingle (see note on page 5), expressive.*

She runs out of steam.

Et cetera.

Beat.

SIHLE. I've never heard that song in my life.

BONOLO. No?

SIHLE. What's it supposed to imply?

BONOLO. It's clever, it's about how they see you. *Saw* you. As this… you bend over backwards. You accommodate. You assume the shape of the environment you're in. That's not a bad thing! It's just how you come across.

SIHLE. And you knew the whole time? What the nickname meant?

BONOLO. Not until the party. Not until that guy confirmed it.

SIHLE *considers this.*

Are you offended?

SIHLE. Just surprised. Just thinking. Is that all he said?

BONOLO. He said you were a good sport. That you never took it personally. I guess it's because you found it funny when they called you the name and then he decided you were a nice guy. A cool guy.

SIHLE. It was a stupid name. I found it funny how stupid it was.

BONOLO. He thought you loved it. Does he still work there?

SIHLE. Lipschitz? They transferred him to the London office. He totalled his Audi last year, broke four ribs and had to have his jaw wired shut.

BONOLO. God.

SIHLE. Had a hand in it, I guess.

BONOLO. Messy. You were the one who laughed at the nickname.

SIHLE. I don't know what you're – ?

BONOLO. He had no idea you didn't like the name, that's not how karma works. People need to have been intentional assholes for it to be karma.

SIHLE. Who made that rule?

BONOLO. God also.

    BONOLO *shrugs*.

SIHLE. So how'd **you** know the song? The Slinky song.

BONOLO. Everyone knows it.

SIHLE. No ordinary black child who grew up in South Africa in the eighties knows that song.

BONOLO. I do.

    SIHLE *makes a face like: point proven*.

    What's that? What's that – (*She imitates his off-handed shrug*.)

SIHLE. I mean of course *you* know it but that's not – (*Off her expression*.) Bonolo, when I met you, you insisted I call you Nolly. You'd never left the Southern Suburbs of Cape Town (except for your annual family vacations to Perth) and you had to google what *iwaskom* was when I told you about it.

BONOLO. Not *all black people* had to bathe in a tin bucket.

SIHLE. But only black people with a full satellite package know what the Slinky song is. And this thing about your cousin Nomfundo's house in the township?

BONOLO. What about it?

SIHLE. You mentioned it to them, how your people live eight to a house. Have you been?

BONOLO. Been what?

SIHLE. To Langa, to that house, to your cousins.

BONOLO. So what if I haven't?

SIHLE. Well.

BONOLO. So what if I haven't, I was making a point, what's yours?

SIHLE. I was the first black guy you dated, the second black friend you had *in your life*. My point is that you've always been bougie as fuck.

Beat.

BONOLO. If you'd already reached that conclusion, why'd you ask?

SIHLE. I'm trying to understand. I'd like to. You clearly have an issue with the shack, with them bringing it up, but *what* are you upset about?

BONOLO. They've never visited us.

SIHLE. No.

BONOLO. You don't find it interesting that their first visit was because of a shack?

SIHLE. That was an aside. A tangent. They came for the cheese.

BONOLO. Stop it.

SIHLE. I'm trying to defuse you, you're about to detonate. What if they wanted to get to know us, as neighbours do?

BONOLO. I've been asking Lyn to come over for months.

SIHLE. Everyone's busy, everyone has a life.

BONOLO. Last time I invited her, you know what she said? They had a golf meet.

SIHLE. Can I ask a question.

BONOLO. What.

SIHLE. Do you want me to be offended?

BONOLO. No.

SIHLE. Then why are you trying to convince me that I should be?

BONOLO. I'm not.

SIHLE. Something about this has you pressed and you want me to be pressed too.

BONOLO. I don't care if you're not pressed.

SIHLE. You can't accept that I may genuinely not be offended by these people.

BONOLO. I understand we can't think the same way.

SIHLE. Good, that's a start.

BONOLO. I just don't understand how you think.

SIHLE. Let's go see the shack.

BONOLO. I know what a *shack* looks like, I don't need to *see* it.

SIHLE. We can't fix it like this.

BONOLO. Fix what?

SIHLE. Any of it. If we're going to figure out how we play this, them, the whole thing, we need to be open to listening to their concerns.

BONOLO. Do the hard part. Right.

SIHLE. *Hayi, angikwazi ukubonisana nawe.*

A little moment.

BONOLO. I don't know what you just said.

SIHLE. I said I can't reason with you.

BONOLO. So why not just say that.

SIHLE. I'm sorry. I forgot.

BONOLO. Bullshit, you forgot. It's a power play.

SIHLE. A power play?

BONOLO. It's a power play, you do it without even noticing, it's subconscious, your lizard brain working. When I have a point and you know it, you snatch the power back by doing *that*.

SIHLE. By speaking?

BONOLO. In Zulu.

SIHLE. Do you feel guilty?

BONOLO. About?

SIHLE. About our life. About what we have.

BONOLO. Why would I feel…

  JESS *comes out in tights and a sports bra.*

  ANDREW *enters too. Gets comfortable, kicks off his shoes.*

  ANDREW *and* JESS *begin to change the decor, replacing the more obvious Afro-centric stuff with some 'shabby chic' pieces. Distressed wood. Neutral pillows. Pretty little vases. A bit twee, but cute if you're into that sort of thing.*
  ANDREW *and* JESS *are.*

  You know you don't have to defend your territory against some squatters. They're not going to take anything from you.

SIHLE. Not yet. Not until we choose how to react. Because that shack, whoever lives there? You don't owe them anything. That truth makes you uncomfortable, and I'm sorry about it.

  But you're part of Stillwater. That's whose side we're on.

  ANDREW *moves to one of the windows, stares out at the shack.* JESS *joins him.*

  JESS *puts a hand on* ANDREW's *shoulder. A tableau as they stare out their window. The lights change and we're with –*

Scene Four

JESS *and* ANDREW, *still looking out.*

JESS *steps away and begins her yoga stretches on the rug.*

ANDREW *keeps looking.*

ANDREW. It's morphing. How?

JESS. I don't even know.

ANDREW. Every time I look, it's changed. Now there are windows. Yesterday there were no windows.

JESS. I guess they need to let the light in.

ANDREW. How've they been here for two weeks and we've never seen them? That thing can't be much bigger than two-by-two, you have to come out some time to, to breathe or...

JESS. Who says they're in there all the time? Maybe it's only overnight.

ANDREW. Then how early do they leave?

JESS. Like, five?

ANDREW. I was up at four-thirty. No one wakes before four-thirty. I mean, one or two days, I get, I get that we'd miss them for a couple of days. Several days. But *fourteen days*?

JESS. Maybe come away from there. Maybe stop looking at it.

ANDREW. It's a kettle, Jess.

JESS. What?

ANDREW. It's a kettle. If I watch it, it won't boil.

JESS. You're obsessed.

ANDREW. It's not like they can tell we're looking. Or do you think they can?

JESS. Maybe that's why they never come out.

ANDREW. I'm going over there.

JESS. Don't go over there.

ANDREW. Why not?

JESS. I don't know it's just – it's not really our business or our place to – they could feel, I dunno, cornered. They could feel attacked, I don't feel like intimidation / will –

ANDREW. I'm the *least* intimidating person I know! There's no person less likely to intimidate anyone than me. I've the casual face of someone who just wants a friendly chat.

JESS *regards him from downward dog.*

JESS. *H-mm.*

ANDREW. *Hmm-mm* what*?*

JESS. Nothing, just obser– babe, can you stop blocking the light. Move. Move from the window.

ANDREW. And it really isn't bothering anyone else. It's like no one else's noticed.

JESS. What did the group say?

ANDREW. Crickets.

JESS. I mentioned it to Chris and Lyn.

ANDREW. Oh yeah? (You didn't tell me that), what did they say?

JESS. Said people around here were the quiet type. Kept to themselves. No one likes to be the first to cause a fuss.

ANDREW. Well that's not news. Two months and they don't give a shit about us. No one's even said hello. Aren't they supposed to bring you pie when you move to the suburbs?

JESS. That's an American thing.

ANDREW. Then they should bring us the equivalent. Curry.

JESS. I'm not eating anyone else's curry, people have nails.

ANDREW. I'll eat the fucking curry.

JESS. They need time to get used to us.

ANDREW. They can tell we don't belong here.

JESS. Based on *what*?

ANDREW. On a feeling I have, it's like a... d'you think we made the right choice? To buy here? Cos I'm starting to feel like we overpaid.

JESS. We got a great price. What you're worried about doesn't exist.

ANDREW. My bank account? That exists.

JESS. What people think of us. What you think people think of us.

ANDREW. I mean they must know just by looking. That we're a little outside our price range here. That we only got this place by pure luck.

JESS. **Who** is thinking about us that much?

ANDREW. The other couple who didn't get the house. They made a higher offer than we did.

JESS. They don't know that.

ANDREW. But Lynette does.

JESS. She liked us, there's no harm in that. The Sharpes are good people.

ANDREW. I'm starting to think they're the only other people who live here. Starting to think all these houses are just for show. I mean, in the morning? When I go to work? It feels like a ghost town.

JESS. Creepy.

ANDREW. That's what I'm fucking – yesterday, I drove really slow. Like, twenty. Tried to get a good look at the houses, maybe I'd see someone getting their mail, watering their garden. Maybe see someone through a window.

JESS. Creepier.

ANDREW. I went all the way around the cul-de-sac, took a left, passed the park, went around the traffic circle, and you know what I saw? *Nothing*. No one walking, no one driving, every window, every door, shut. The only open window was on that billboard, the one they haven't taken down. 'Stillwater: Coming Soon.' I mean surely, by now, it's come. We're here. Do you think people are avoiding us?

JESS. Chris said people keep to themselves.

ANDREW. Fucking pretentious.

JESS. You're making stuff up. No one has an issue with us, this is a natural part of settling into a new neighbourhood.

ANDREW. We should've stayed in Woodstock.

JESS. Ay no, come, you don't miss that dump. Remember the sound of the rats in the ceiling.

JESS *makes a drumming-scrabbling sound on the floor, like rats scuttling*.

ANDREW. Stop that, my PTSD's flaring up.

JESS. Stop second-guessing us.

ANDREW. What do you see out there, do you ever see anyone when you're doing your yoga stuff?

JESS. Cul-de-sac's not really high on the foot traffic –

ANDREW. Right.

JESS. – and we're facing an empty plot of land, so.

ANDREW. What else did Chris say?

JESS. Basically he said, if we were to get some support, like wanted the neighbourhood to get fired up about doing something, taking this thing seriously, it would take some work.

We'd have to, I guess, find people who agree with us. He said he'd been thinking about it for a while. That Stillwater needed some sort of Neighbourhood Watch. To keep an eye.

ANDREW. And does Chris?

JESS. Does Chris what?

ANDREW. Agree with us. Agree that it's reasonable to serve an eviction order.

JESS. Mostly.

ANDREW. And the other bit?

JESS. The other bit is optics.

ANDREW. Optics being...

JESS. How it looks, *shit*, you're so anxious, I can't chaturanga with you here, you're bringing this negative energy into – why are you home so early?

ANDREW. No reason.

JESS. Make yourself useful, at least? Come stretch my shoulder.

ANDREW *goes behind, holds onto* JESS*'s elbow. She leans into the stretch with a groan.* ANDREW*'s a little turned on by it, not gonna lie. He forgets himself for a moment there, pushes a little harder.* JESS *groans some more.*

ANDREW *kind of likes it, grows a touch more forceful. Encouraged by her feedback, he uses his knee on her shoulder, takes off his T-shirt.* JESS *doesn't notice until the shirt drops on the floor beside her.*

Oh – what? – no. No no no no.

ANDREW. I thought you were –

JESS. That I was what?

ANDREW. Inviting me to – never mind.

JESS. Did I make it seem like...

ANDREW. You said I was anxious, I thought you were – I'll put it back on.

ANDREW *scrambles back into his T-shirt. It's awkward now. They kind of avoid each other's eyes.* JESS *softens.*

JESS. Hey. *Hey.*

They draw in again. Hug. A sort of truce.

Guess what.

ANDREW. What.

JESS. I unpacked the last box today.

ANDREW. We're settled?

JESS. We're settlers.

ANDREW. I'm proud of us.

JESS. Me too.

ANDREW. A place of our own.

JESS. Finally.

ANDREW. Thanks to you. You're the reason we got it.

JESS. You keep saying that.

ANDREW. Lyn liked you.

JESS. We got along.

ANDREW. You won her over and she caved. People are
    powerless in the face of your charm.

JESS. I know you are.

ANDREW. I am.

*Something's about to happen when the doorbell goes. Both
share a look.*

You have a client now?

JESS. Not till this evening. Delivery?

*ANDREW shrugs, heads to the door. JESS goes back to her
stretches. ANDREW opens. It's BONOLO and SIHLE. Both
in baggy workout clothes, looking slightly sweaty and
unkempt. BONOLO's a bit tight about this.*

Who's there?

SIHLE. *Hiiii.*

ANDREW. Hi?

SIHLE. Sihle Mbatha.

ANDREW. Andrew Fraser…

JESS. Who's there?

ANDREW. I'm trying to figure that out.

SIHLE. Hi, sorry, we haven't met. We're your new neighbours.
This is my wife Bonolo.

ANDREW. Oh. *Oh.*

   JESS *grabs a hand towel, heads to the door.*

JESS. Hi there?

ANDREW. Babe this is… Sihle and – Bonolo, was it?

BONOLO. Right.

JESS. Okay, hi.

ANDREW. They said they were our – you said you were our
new neighbours?

SIHLE. Well we've been here for a while. But relatively
speaking, to you, new. Yes. Hi.

JESS. Okay. Well do you want to come inside? I'm sorry, the
place is a bit of a mess, but you're welcome to come inside.

SIHLE. Sorry to just barge in like this.

ANDREW. No, not at all. We were – I mean in a manner of
speaking, we were expecting you.

BONOLO. You were?

ANDREW. We knew you'd come over eventually. We didn't
know when. We just hoped –

JESS. We hoped you'd –

BONOLO. I'm so glad. So glad we're not interrupting. We were
out for our afternoon jog and Sihle saw the car in the driveway

and he, *we*, thought, why not. Today's as good a day as any to come over, introduce ourselves.

JESS. You jog?

SIHLE. We try.

ANDREW. That is so… *wow*. I've never seen you out there.

BONOLO. It's not a daily thing. We've got it down to once a week now.

JESS. Ah-*ha*.

BONOLO. So this was enough exercise until well into next week.

ANDREW. Right. Next week? Great.

Now what?

SIHLE. So Chris Sharpe came to talk to us. You obviously must know –

ANDREW. He did?

SIHLE. About your little issue.

JESS. Oh wow, okay, I didn't think he'd, I mean I didn't ask him to do that. I didn't ask him to intervene.

BONOLO. Do you mind that he –

JESS. No no, not really, no. I just mentioned it to him as an aside I didn't think he'd go so far as to ask you about it. Directly.

BONOLO. *I* get it.

ANDREW. I mean, it's good that he did. It kind of breaks the ice for us. For all of us.

SIHLE. I think so too.

JESS. What exactly did he say?

BONOLO. That you guys took issue with the shack.

ANDREW. *Oh.* Look we don't want to offend anyone. An issue, sure, you could call it that…

BONOLO. Or?

ANDREW. Or…

BONOLO. It sounded like you were about to say 'or'.

ANDREW. No. That was the end of the sentence. An issue. You could call it that. Full stop.

JESS. Can I get you guys anything? Water?

BONOLO. That would actually be great. I'd love that.

JESS. Lemme get that for you.

JESS *flees to the kitchen.* ANDREW *kind of shifts his weight from one foot to the other.*

BONOLO. Can I just ask? Up front. What is your problem with the shack?

ANDREW. Okay – we're doing this now? – fine, I can uh…

BONOLO. Nobody's hurting anyone. The shack itself isn't hurting you. It's not your land, as I understand, it's a no-man's-land. It's not being used.

SIHLE. Give him a chance to –

BONOLO. I'm giving, I'm asking. What's the harm?

ANDREW. The harm – Jess, those waters?

JESS. They're coming.

BONOLO. What's the harm because as far as we understand, it's nobody's –

ANDREW. Yeah, we get that. And it may seem like that presents an open invitation (shall we close this?) it may seem like an open invitation but –

BONOLO. It's not.

ANDREW. No. Exactly.

JESS *returns with two glasses of tap water. Offers them to* BONOLO *and* SIHLE. *Both drink.* ANDREW *and* JESS *wait for them to finish. Share a glance or two.*

Are you some sort of activist, or is this out of real need?

What?

You must be super-invested or else you wouldn't have – you have your reasons for everything, I'm sure. You seem to feel strongly about it.

BONOLO. I guess I do.

ANDREW. But you're not an –

BONOLO. An activist? No. I have a job.

ANDREW. You do?

JESS. That's nice. Me too. I teach yoga.

Cool.

BONOLO. I hope you don't think I'm being unreasonable. I'm just trying to understand your reservations before we get hysterical.

ANDREW. That's not a danger. I don't think anyone is hysterical.

BONOLO. (Not yet.)

SIHLE. I'm sorry we had to meet because of this, because of an emotional issue. It would've been nicer to meet on more relaxed terms.

ANDREW. Which terms would those have been?

JESS. You mean for a drink / or a –

SIHLE. Exactly. Exactly.

JESS. – a braai or something.

SIHLE. Correct.

BONOLO. That would've been more pleasant, yes.

ANDREW. Why would we – a braai, why would we have met for a braai?

JESS (*obviously*). Because we're neighbours, neighbours do that sometimes. Maybe not in Stillwater. But I mean, Chris did say people mostly kept to themselves here.

SIHLE. (They / tend to do that.)

ANDREW. Yes, no, but not really, we're not really neighbours, are we?

BONOLO. Well we're not right next door but, neighbours just the same.

ANDREW. Guys, everyone, can we just cut the bullshit? I've been trying to keep it polite here, but can we just cut the bullshit and be honest right now? We Are Not Neighbours. Let's start there.

JESS. (Andrew, what the –)

ANDREW. (No, Jess, come on.) I'm trying to have an honest conversation here. Up front, like you said. But we are not neighbours. Let's stop referring to each other as that.

SIHLE. Did I say something wrong?

JESS. No, Sihle.

ANDREW. Neighbours implies you live next door or adjacent to me, separated by a fence or a, a boundary of some sort, in your own *house* with a *roof* and a *door* and *four walls*, and a backyard and uh, maybe a dog, maybe. Your own space, d'you know what I mean?

Everyone's hella confused.

SIHLE (*with a smile*). Well… we do have those things. Not the dog. Bonolo's allergic. But all the other stuff.

ANDREW. No! *No*. That thing, across the way? That piece of… that's not a house. It's not a house, it's not an official dwelling, *please*, it's not a property. It's a piece of tin that you two *cobbled together* on *stolen land*.

Just like that, all the air leaves the room.

JESS. *Jesus Chri–* you're not serious.

ANDREW. What. *What?* Am I lying?

JESS. This is Bonolo and Sihle Mbatha. They **are** our
    neighbours. They live next door to Chris and Lynn. On Boyd
    Street. In Stillwater. In a house. That they own.

    ANDREW *reels.*

ANDREW. W…
    W…
    But you came about the…
    You said you were from the…

BONOLO. From the?

JESS. (Jesus, babe.)

ANDREW. You knew?

JESS. Knew what?

ANDREW. That they weren't the people!

SIHLE. Which people?

JESS. Of course I knew.

ANDREW. *How?!*

BONOLO. Maybe this wasn't the best time…

ANDREW. How'd you know?

JESS. The… I heard them speak, I heard the… accents, Chris
    mentioned they were… Jesus…

BONOLO. Maybe we should've called or – been clearer when
    we introduced ourselves.

JESS. No, no, I understood, I knew perfectly well who you
    were, it's just…

BONOLO. We're not usually dressed like this, we were
    jogging –

JESS. *Of course*, it makes sense, I'm absolutely – oh my god, Andrew –

SIHLE *begins to laugh. Apropos of nothing and no one. The sound takes everyone by surprise because yes, it's oddly placed. The rest kind of just stare at him while he does this.* ANDREW *chuckles along, trying to figure out what this laughter means for him.*

JESS *cracks a smile.* SIHLE*'s laughter is just too infectious not to.*

ANDREW *starts to join in the laughter. Getting into it now. It's growing.*

SIHLE *wipes tears from his eyes, highly amused. Extraordinarily amused.* BONOLO *has a smile too, but its cool precision is aimed at* SIHLE *only.*

SIHLE *calms himself down.* JESS *and* ANDREW*'s laughter dies down too, slowly. It's like we've opened a pressure valve. Some of the tension now alleviated as –*

SIHLE. Listen, it was an honest mistake.

JESS. It's *mortifying*.

BONOLO. I'm sure.

ANDREW. Yes. Yes it is. God, I am *so* sorry.

SIHLE. Don't mention it.

ANDREW. Can we begin again?

SIHLE. I'm not offended.

JESS. I think you have every reason to be offended. He confused you with... confused you for...

BONOLO. Some other black people!

ANDREW. *Jesus.*

BONOLO. I sometimes get white people mixed up. Y'all look the same too.

JESS. Ha-ha.

BONOLO. I keep reintroducing myself to the same white women, so I get your predicament. And Sihle understands it's not personal. He understands that mistakes happen, he's a good sport about these kind of things, right Slinky?

SIHLE *reacts to that – subtle*.

SIHLE. Right.

JESS. Okay. Let's just begin again.

BONOLO. Hello. I'm Bonolo and this is Sihle, we're the Mbathas. We're over on Boyd Street, number sixteen.

JESS. I'm Jess and this is Welcome to our house.

ANDREW (*genuinely trying*). So nice to meet you. Neighbours.

BONOLO. Likewise.

JESS. Andrew and I had started to wonder if anyone else lived here.

SIHLE. And now you know.

JESS. It's honestly such a relief to see other people.

BONOLO. So do you two have any kids?

JESS. No, you?

BONOLO. Not yet.

JESS. And you guys have lived here for –

BONOLO. Two years.

JESS. Wow. So you got in early. Pioneers. Did Lyn sell you the house too?

BONOLO. We came before she took over the sales for Stillwater.

JESS. And do you like it?

BONOLO. It was one of our better decisions. Stillwater felt… right. A good place to live, to raise a family in, a community

we could grow into, integrate into, grow with, that would grow
into us. A protected investment, does that make any sense?

JESS. Yes, perfect – we felt that too, didn't we, babe?

ANDREW. Yeah.

JESS. It's aspirational, I guess. Not necessarily who we are
now, but who we'd like to be. Do you know what sold us? It
was the fact that there were no walls. That it was just lawn,
open space, no fences separating us from each other. No
worries about whether we're safe. What freedom.

ANDREW. Those kinds of worries are always there, of course.

JESS. Yeah but you don't get this kind of safety anywhere.

ANDREW. The safest town is an empty town.

BONOLO. Ha.

JESS. Anyway, it's a relief, so good to see other friendly faces.

ANDREW. Just, if you don't mind me asking this, how much
did you guys… buy in for?

JESS. (Andrew*wwww*.)

ANDREW. Is that an inappropriate question?

SIHLE. You mean for our house?

ANDREW. You don't have to answer if you don't want to.

JESS. Andrew's been *obsessing* over – I'm so sorry –

BONOLO. Not at all, we don't mind, I think it was two-point…

SIHLE. Six? Two-point-five, two-point-six. Something like that.

ANDREW. Wow.

JESS. Okay. Wow.

SIHLE. Why, how much did you –

ANDREW. Oh nowhere close to that.

SIHLE. How much?

ANDREW. Three-point-five.

BONOLO. Million –

ANDREW. – million Rand, yes. Million*s*.

SIHLE. We got in early.

ANDREW. Early's good. Early is good. If you sold now that would be a **solid** profit my friend.

SIHLE. We weren't thinking of selling, but that's good / to know –

BONOLO. *Three-point-five?*

SIHLE. – it's good to know the going rate is going up.

JESS. It's worth it, I think. Anyway, we wouldn't have been able to buy in when you did, this would've been way out of our range.

ANDREW. It's *still* way out of our range. If Jess hadn't charmed Lyn…

JESS. Okay, not charmed. We developed a rapport. She liked me, I liked her, we got the house.

ANDREW. We haven't eaten in three months but hey, we have a house.

BONOLO. Oh, shit. Are you…?

ANDREW. No it's a joke. I'm joking. We've eaten.

BONOLO. Ha!

ANDREW. It's a joke about how broke we are.

JESS. In poor taste.

ANDREW. No pun intended. Sorry.

SIHLE. Chris says you have a restaurant?

ANDREW. Manage –

SIHLE. Manage a restaurant.

ANDREW. It's a hole in the wall, we make artisan sandwiches. High quality, good ingredients, limited menu options. Bread.

BONOLO. And how's that going?

ANDREW. Terribly.

JESS. Andrew'd like to give you the impression that everything in our lives is unequivocally shit.

SIHLE. Doing well so far.

ANDREW. Is that how I'm coming across? Sheesh, sorry.

BONOLO. No need to be optimistic on our account.

ANDREW. Forgive me, I'm usually quite chirpy. It's just this shack thing has me stressed out.

Everyone accepts.

SIHLE. So look – to get to the issue at hand.

JESS. Oh god, right, that's why you're here.

ANDREW. Have you... seen it?

BONOLO. We didn't go right *up* to it but yes. We saw it from your porch.

ANDREW. Come have a look here.

ANDREW goes to the window. Gestures at SIHLE to join. SIHLE reluctantly does so. Grits at BONOLO to follow. She does.

I mean it's really detailed, isn't it? That doesn't look temporary to me. Does it look temporary to you?

SIHLE. No.

ANDREW. This is my thing. It looks like they're getting comfortable. Like they've really settled in.

SIHLE. Uh-huh. So they have.

During the following bit, JESS will join them at the 'window'.

So will LYNETTE *and* CHRIS.

ANDREW. See how they've painted the front door, painted the window frames? That wasn't there just now. It's like every time we look away, there's more to it. They keep taking up more space, creeping outwards. Today a painted door, tomorrow a second floor, a balcony, a satellite dish...

JESS. Some plants, maybe a vegetable garden. When they pin themselves down with stuff it makes it more difficult to move them.

LYNETTE. Precisely. Then it's just sort of oh, they're part of the environment now. They live here because there's a lock on the door, there's a welcome mat at the entrance, there's glass in the panes.

CHRIS. And soon there are two of them. Three. Four. It's gradual. You stop noticing it. Like nails growing.

And lo and behold, somehow – without us really noticing – the shadowy shack has germinated a satellite dish on its roof, a potted plant beside the door, a rusty bicycle leaning against its side.

The lights changing as we slide into the next scene...

ANDREW. And once they've been here long enough, they're no longer squatters. Then they're simply. Neighbours.

BONOLO *sings the Slinky song as we slide into –*

Scene Five

BONOLO *and* SIHLE *in their house.* BONOLO *continues to sing.*

SIHLE. Really?

    BONOLO *sings.*

    Are you done?

    BONOLO *keeps singing.*

    That's hilarious to you.

BONOLO. Not as hilarious as Andrew was to you, the way you laughed just then?

SIHLE. Yeah fine, chill.

BONOLO. Was that to relieve the tension in general or to make him feel less awkward?

SIHLE. Neither, I just wasn't fussed. It was amusing.

BONOLO. It was *hmm* amusing, not *har-har* amusing.

SIHLE. He was embarrassed, that was payback enough.

BONOLO. You did the thing with your mouth though.

SIHLE. What thing, I / didn't –

BONOLO. Yeah, the twitch, the little twitch at the corner of your mouth, you do it when you're bothered.

SIHLE. You don't know my expressions as well as you think.

BONOLO. Your determined cheerfulness in the face of bullshit, Sihle, happens to be what I admire most about you.

    She chuckles some more.

SIHLE. Briggs needs me on a call, should we order in?

BONOLO. I'll get the med bowl from the usual place, sauce on the side, extra avo. I'll go fetch it at the boom gate. You found Andrew's slip-up funny, really?

SIHLE. That's hard to believe?

BONOLO. You make that face when your Aunt Nobuhle says
a proud Zulu man would have six children by now.

SIHLE *bristles*.

See?! There! That twitch.

SIHLE. It's your imagination.

BONOLO. Jess seems nice.

SIHLE. Plain.

BONOLO. She was mortified, I liked it. But she might've made
the same mistake if the Sharpes hadn't told her we were black.

SIHLE. You will *not* give anyone the benefit of doubt.

BONOLO. Also – aside? That house costs way too much for the
insides to look like an Airbnb from 2012.

SIHLE. You're a snob.

BONOLO. I have exceptional taste. They paid *three-point-five*?

SIHLE. Don't be so smug about it.

BONOLO. We made a million profit in two years.

SIHLE. It's only profit when you sell.

BONOLO. And you know what profit gets you? *Freedom*. I'm
gonna go get the food.

SIHLE. They'll deliver to the door.

BONOLO. It takes no time for me to walk up there.

SIHLE. It's more convenient for them to bring it.

BONOLO. I'll just take the walk, yeah?

SIHLE *realises*.

SIHLE. You're going to see the shack.

BONOLO. No.

SIHLE. Wait-wait, no, you want to walk over there and go see it.

BONOLO. First of all, you're making it seem as if you caught me out.

SIHLE. Why would you go look at it without me?

BONOLO. Second of all –

SIHLE. There's no second of all.

BONOLO. I want to know what it is up close.

SIHLE. What do you think you'll find?

BONOLO. I want to make up my own mind.

SIHLE. You already have. According to you, everyone's overreacting and we should all just stand by while our community is invaded.

BONOLO *thinks*.

BONOLO. Tell me. Is this all you've ever wanted?

SIHLE (*weary*). *Yes* Bonolo, this moment is all I could've dreamed of.

BONOLO. Here, where we are, what we've achieved, what we've become, what we *have*. Is this it, for you?

SIHLE. Where's this coming – no, of course this isn't *it*. This isn't *all* there is, ever. Isn't it Solon who said, call no man happy until he is dead?

BONOLO. We're spouting the Greeks now are we.

SIHLE. What are you getting at?

BONOLO. That this thing about life where... we gather. We gather all the things, we buy them, we accumulate. And then we protect the things we gather, we put them behind walls or put locks on them and we call it *mine*. Ours.

SIHLE. Yeah that's exactly what it is, welcome.

BONOLO. I never wanted to be that.

SIHLE. Me and you, we knew what we had to do to get ahead. That's how we got this life. Make friends, be good colleagues, yeah? A good neighbour, good citizen, not take ourselves too seriously. Be helpful, be in solidarity, pay our taxes...

BONOLO. Sure, you're very helpful. But I'm to believe it's all a tactic? To what end?

SIHLE. If you like them so much, your friends in the shack, invite them over.

BONOLO. I'm asking, to what end.

SIHLE. Just invite them over, to live here. With us.

BONOLO. You're being deliberately / obtuse.

SIHLE. We have the room. We have three bedrooms, it's more space than we'll ever need. Seeing how we're all the same in your eyes, the oppressed masses, let whoever those people are come join us.

BONOLO. *Those people* have a house. It's over there.

SIHLE. It's not a particularly good one.

BONOLO. They shouldn't have to leave where they are because this neighbourhood considers them a threat.

SIHLE. You don't believe they're a threat.

BONOLO. Of course not.

SIHLE. So why won't you let them in **your** house.

BONOLO. Because they're strangers, Sihle.

SIHLE. Not *dangerous* strangers, according to you. They're like us. So you shouldn't be afraid of them.

BONOLO. You're getting defensive when the point I'm trying to make is –

SIHLE. If you're such a *good person* then you shouldn't be opposed to giving away what we have, some of what we have, to them.

BONOLO. Let's just drop it.

SIHLE. To the people who have nothing, you don't want to offer your cheese knife? You don't want to offer them a pillow for their bed, a champagne glass? Or what, that's **too** close to home.

BONOLO. I will. I can. Will it make you happy? Here. I'll take it over there right now. Two cushions. This vase. This paperweight. That work for you?

SIHLE. I'm sure they'd really appreciate a hand-blown glass paperweight from Murano.

BONOLO. Will it make you happy, if I *perform* for you that I actually *do* give a fuck?

SIHLE. What does it have to do with *me*? I'm just trying to determine why

BONOLO. No-no you're not trying to determine anything, you're trying to tie me in knots, to play some sort of gotcha game, to catch me out when I say the slightest contradiction – the thing, the thing where you try and snuff out inconsistencies, you're trying to see where, how far I'll bend.

SIHLE. *You're saying* they have a right to illegally occupy any property, just not your property.

You're *saying* they have a right to any stuff, just not your stuff.

You're saying they're *like us*, except in all the ways they aren't.

SIHLE. I'm trying to see how many ways you can twist before you snap.

BONOLO. You know what you lack? It's empathy.

SIHLE *reels*.

SIHLE. I lack…?

BONOLO. Empathy, yes, the ability to care for those less fortunate than yourself. When did you become so *selfish*, so protective of your little mound of dirt?

SIHLE. When I *paid* for that mound of fucking dirt. I am more like the people in that shack than you'll ever be.

BONOLO. And that upsets you most of all, does it?

SIHLE. Yes. *Yes!* I ran hard to be free of them, of people like them, I put so much distance between that *thing* out there and myself, so much *work* went into outrunning the memory of how I used to go to school smelling of the open coal fire we burned at home for heat, about how I got called all sorts of names *worse* than Slinky for riding a bicycle made of scrap, for my second-hand clothes, for my house full of people who slept on mattresses on the floor, only for that *motherfucker* to confuse me for –

BONOLO. Ah-*hah*, so it did bother you!

SIHLE. What bothers me is that shack's **existence** getting in the way of what I made, the life I made. I've struggled enough.

BONOLO. Oh *please*, you use your difficult upbringing like chips in a casino, slamming it on the table as and when it suits you. But in fact you'd prefer to be inoffensively invisible. Don't mind the shadow in the corner.

SIHLE. You perform your blackness to soothe your conscience.

BONOLO. You want to fit so badly you're willing to erase yourself if it gets you the approval you so desperately crave.

SIHLE. You'd rather die than admit you've not struggled a day in your life.

BONOLO. You think by working harder you can replace 'blackness' as your defining characteristic? You think you can outrun their prejudice by taking their side? You can't bear being mistaken for what you actually are. *A black man*.

SIHLE. Your comfort is your boundary line. God forbid you have to put action behind your rhetoric. God forbid you have to stand behind the loudspeaker you yell through. You can't do both, you can't be an activist on the side of 'take back the land' and have a fence protecting your good life and your house and your *stuff*. You're not free, you live in a world of walls, **that's** the world you've chosen. You're not a revolutionary, you're a capitalist.

BONOLO *is silent. Then –*

BONOLO. I'm going to fetch the food.

BONOLO *goes.*

BONOLO*'s gone, leaving* SIHLE *alone.*

Without him noticing, another part of the shack begins to sprout and grow.

As the lights change, he walks into –

Scene Six

Andrew and Jess's house. Everyone seated. SIHLE *takes a seat too.*

CHRIS. So, with that, everyone, welcome. To the, uh, first gathering of the Stillwater Concerned Residents Group. Uh, the Wilsons send their apologies. Number twelve, the McIntyres, out of town –

LYNETTE. (Daughter's graduation.)

CHRIS. – but reiterated they support the decisions made in this forum. David and Elena will join us as soon as their babysitter pitches. Luckily I can no longer relate.

Polite chuckles.

(*To* SIHLE.) We're missing…

SIHLE. She'll be here in a moment, go right ahead.

CHRIS. Great. Well okay, this shouldn't take too long. Like I said, just an introduction and a first meeting for this association or, group, let's just call it a group. Thank you Jess and Andrew for your generous offer to host us and the, uh, spread.

BONOLO slips in without fanfare.

ANDREW. Yeah, no problem.

JESS. Happy to. Help yourselves everyone.

LYNETTE. Oh I'll jump right in, looks gorgeous, this. Did you make it yourself?

JESS. It's from the Spar.

LYNETTE. Ah. Anyone else for a slice?

Everyone politely declines. LYNETTE*'s stuck with whatever it is.*

CHRIS. Okay so to the first order of business, yes? I've taken the liberty of drawing up the eviction order, Lyn and I have, and um… have a look at that and let us know. We tried to keep the wording civil but firm. You know, like we mean business. Which we absolutely do.

CHRIS hands SIHLE a sheaf of paper. SIHLE reads it over.

JESS, LYNETTE, CHRIS and ANDREW watch him do this. SIHLE notices he's being watched, shifts uncomfortably.

At that, JESS, CHRIS, LYNETTE *and* ANDREW *disperse.*

BONOLO peers over SIHLE*'s shoulder to read the document too.*

SIHLE. Sorry, we're just –

CHRIS. No, take your time. No rush.

SIHLE and BONOLO take their time. The others wait. Finally:

All in order?

BONOLO. I have one question.

CHRIS. What's that?

BONOLO. It only has our names to be signed? At the bottom here.

LYNETTE. We thought it would be best if –

CHRIS. More targeted –

LYNETTE. More targeted, right, if it came from one place.

BONOLO *looks to* SIHLE *for his reaction.* SIHLE *only nods.*

SIHLE. Okay.

LYNETTE. Okay? Fantastic.

BONOLO. I have one more question.

CHRIS. Fire.

BONOLO. Under 'reasons for request of eviction'.

'I, the undersigned...' et cetera et cetera, '...feel that your structure affects my freedom of movement and has made me fear for my personal safety...' I... that's not it. Is it?

LYNETTE. No, we know it's a broad generalisation of the –

BONOLO. That's *really* not it. Can we remove that?

CHRIS. Go ahead.

BONOLO. Does anyone have a –

JESS. Pen, here you go.

ANDREW. Can we remove the 'freedom of movement' bit and keep the 'fear for personal safety' bit?

BONOLO. Why?

ANDREW. I just feel like, you know, it's correct.

BONOLO. You feel afraid?

ANDREW. I think I do.

BONOLO. You can't *think* you do. Do you or do you not feel –

ANDREW. Okay, alright, I do, I feel afraid for my personal safety. And you don't have to tell me that's unreasonable, I get it. There may not be any real danger. I may be projecting.

LYNETTE. I think we understand. It's how you feel, you have every right –

BONOLO. But my name is on this document.

CHRIS. Bonolo is right. If her and Sihle have to sign, they're the ones who should be comfortable with the wording.

BONOLO. So I can – ?

CHRIS. You can strike it out.

    BONOLO *does*.

SIHLE. I think that's it then.

CHRIS. Great!

LYNETTE. Well I, for one, will be relieved to see the back of this.

JESS. You and me both.

LYNETTE. I can't help but feel that this has upset our ecosystem, it's unbalanced us all. I want things to go back to how they were. Back to normal.

SIHLE. So do we.

ANDREW. So what are the next steps?

CHRIS. Well – the first steps. The Mbathas will go and talk to them, to the occupiers, and serve them this notice.

JESS. The first, why do you say the first?

CHRIS. There's a procedure here. After we've spoken to them, and if they refuse to move, we submit these documents to the court. They'll be given an opportunity to respond and oppose the eviction –

ANDREW. Whoa, whoa, whoa – to *oppose*?

LYNETTE. That is, unfortunately, the information we were given.

ANDREW. How long can this go on for?

CHRIS. Well once they've been given that opportunity, they'll receive a Section Forty-Two notice to appear in court. They – and we – will present our cases. The judge will then either postpone the case –

LYNETTE. If the squatters don't have legal counsel –

CHRIS. Right, and if they do, the judge will decide if an eviction is indeed legal, based on the case made by the municipality, after which an eviction order may be issued to the occupiers and they'll be given time to move. If they haven't moved by a certain date, the eviction will then be carried out.

ANDREW. *How long can this go on for?*

LYNETTE. All accounted for… up to six months. Conservatively.

ANDREW. Conservatively?!

CHRIS. I know it seems unreasonable –

ANDREW. Six *fucking* months?

JESS. Babe, calm down.

ANDREW. I can't take this. I can't take much more of it. Every cent we have is tied up in this property. If it loses so much as a *fraction* of its value because of that goddamn –

LYNETTE. No, Andrew, no, we're getting in ahead of this.

ANDREW. Because in the nextneighbourhoodover, Lyn –

CHRIS. No, we're not letting it get that far.

ANDREW. Have you looked out there recently, have you seen how much that thing's grown?

LYNETTE. It is a bit of a weed.

ANDREW. And it's just the beginning, that's how it began for them. When you sold us this house –

CHRIS. Now, Andrew –

ANDREW. When you sold us this house, it was with the promise of a safe, picturesque – no one said anything about an eyesore of a – you said it was an investment, that the property would *increase* –

LYNETTE. There's no way I could've / predicted –

BONOLO. Your property value is not going to plummet because of one little tin house on a –

LYNETTE. Actually, yes, it will.

BONOLO. No, it won't.

ANDREW. And you know what it'll be, six months from now? Twenty of them and three live animals under one roof, burning fires indoors, playing god knows what music all hours of the day, a patched-together, three-bedroom, two-bathroom duplex made of tin with a blow-up pool and a fucking granny flat!

Everyone takes a moment after this outburst. BONOLO *recovers first.*

BONOLO. And you wouldn't consider what you just described to be a good house, would you Andrew?

ANDREW. A what?

BONOLO. A good house. A place where respectable, decent people reside.

ANDREW. No decent people would take what doesn't belong to them, you must agree.

BONOLO. Nor squeeze twenty under one roof, or burn fires indoors, or play loud music or any of that sort of thing?

ANDREW. Those were examples, meant to illustrate a –

BONOLO. Yeah I know what an *example* is, I'm just curious about the example you *chose*. Because the house you described is one Sihle would be very familiar with. Right, Sihle?

SIHLE. This has nothing to do with me.

BONOLO. It has everything to do with you.

LYNETTE. Is everything okay?

JESS. Anyone want a plate? Maybe spike the glucose levels a bit.

CHRIS. No thanks Jess.   LYNETTE. Not for me,
                                                              thanks.

ANDREW. Fine, maybe the example I used was misjudged. My apologies, Sihle, if you took offence to that.

SIHLE. Why would I?

ANDREW. I dunno, your wife seems to think it hit close to home or whatever.

BONOLO. Not close, but *in*. *In* the home, in fact, that Sihle grew up in. A home that looked very much, didn't it Sihle, like the one we're trying to get rid of, the one Andrew just described?

SIHLE. What are you doing?

LYNETTE. I don't think it's fair to shame Sihle for –

BONOLO. *Shame?* What about the home Andrew just described feels like shame to you? Tell me. Is it something Sihle *should* be ashamed of?

LYNETTE. Oh no come on, I don't know *where* this is headed. Bonolo, I really didn't take you for –

CHRIS. Can we all get back to the question of the document, we need the signatures on the eviction order, we need the Mbathas to deliver the document.

BONOLO. We'll get to the document, Chris.

SIHLE. Are we, to you? Are we?

ANDREW. Are you *what*…?

SIHLE. Bonolo and I, ARE WE?

ANDREW *rolls that around in his head. Trick question? He can't decide. Everyone waits for his answer. Expectant.*

He finally lands on something.

ANDREW. If you're asking whether I think you're good people… the answer is yes.

SIHLE. That's not what I'm asking. Are we, to you, like the people, the invisible people, the invaders, in that shack? Is the idea of them, to you, exactly like the idea of me? That's what I'm asking.

CHRIS. Is this a conversation worth having?

SIHLE. I think it is. We're having it.

CHRIS. But you haven't ever felt otherwise, have you? You haven't ever felt that we, that this community, don't think of you as good people?

SIHLE. Not explicitly.

JESS. So then why ask him that?

SIHLE. It was a question about how much change, how much assimilation, how much blending, before that house out there is good enough to be part of Stillwater?

CHRIS. No amount of –   LYNETTE. If you guys have
                                objections to signing the
                                paperwork…

BONOLO. We don't. We said we'd sign.

JESS (*very kindly*). Can I be honest? Everyone's trying to fit in, no one belongs, we all have to do a little bit of pretending. I feel like Andrew and I are being made out to be the bad guys here. I don't know why, it is because we noticed the shack? Because we asked for something to be done about it? What else should we have done?

ANDREW. I guess left it. To sprout.

JESS. We, Andrew and I, we're not the gatekeepers. Actually, **you** are.

BONOLO. Us?

JESS. You. That feeling, that itch of discomfort? It's not a feeling you have exclusive rights to. You can't claim it. I'm sick of trying to negotiate all of this *so* delicately. We want to be part of Stillwater, badly, that's why we moved here, but now I don't want to speak in case I say something wrong, by accident, hurt someone's feelings.

LYNETTE. I'm sorry you've felt this way, Jess. I'm sorry you've felt there are gatekeepers in this community. That's not how we want anyone to feel.

ANDREW. But we do. And there are.

SIHLE. It's not us. We aren't the gatekeepers.

ANDREW. Oh, come – the truth is, you have great jobs, you make more money than us, fine. Look at your house. Have you looked at your house?

SIHLE. Yes, it's like yours, but you paid more. So how **does** a yoga teacher and a broke sandwich-shop manager afford a property for over three million? Balance me.

ANDREW. You two have *crystal wine glasses* for fuckssakes.

SIHLE. How do you know that?

ANDREW. They told me! / What does it matter how I know?

SIHLE. Why were our wine glasses a point of discussion?

JESS. (Lyn mentioned it in passing, she said she loved your home –)

LYNETTE. (I said I loved your home, that you had good taste.)

ANDREW. It doesn't *matter*, point is, if you want to talk hierarchies? Social pecking orders? Stillwater's a food chain and you're all at the top of it.

SIHLE. And it's a performance.

CHRIS. (If we could get back to the matter at hand...)

SIHLE. All of it, it's all a performance, I'm always performing, *I* am a performance. Performing my civility, my education, my class, my manners, my money, because if I don't, you'll confuse me for any other black man.

ANDREW. You said you weren't offended by that.

SIHLE. I've said a lot of things.

ANDREW. You really want us to believe that you're outside the gates now? That you're begging to be let in, like us?

JESS. It's not a fucking competition, Andrew.

ANDREW. I just want to be sure I understand. Because all I see are people, not black people, but *people*, who, can I just say, seem to have it pretty good.

SIHLE. Oh you don't *see us as black people*. What are we then?

CHRIS. Easy, you two.

ANDREW. You as well, Chris.

CHRIS. Me what?

ANDREW. This was your idea. Get the Mbathas involved? Manage the optics? God forbid you fall on the wrong side of the PC line. Best to be racist in private, where nobody knows. You people manage it all so finely, who's inside, who's not. How many times did I have to ask to be let into the WhatsApp group?

LYNETTE. What do you mean, 'you people'?

SIHLE. Which WhatsApp group?

ANDREW. The Stillwater one.

SIHLE. There's a WhatsApp group?

LYNETTE. Andrew, who is 'you people'?

ANDREW. No come on, don't turn this into something it's not, you know what I meant –

SIHLE. Who's on the WhatsApp group?

JESS. Oh, dear lord...

ANDREW. Chris added me. I don't know the people, I don't know who's on it. Chris added me.

CHRIS (*weakly*). It's an update group.

SIHLE. Updates about what?

CHRIS. *Community* updates, it's nothing formal it's –

SIHLE. A coupla old friends shooting shit?

LYNETTE. Don't be offended.

BONOLO. How about you let him decide that?

SIHLE. So our 'optics' are good enough but we can't be part of Stillwater's chit-chat?

JESS. I, is any of this important? We are going *so* far off-track right now.

BONOLO. Eat some cake, Jess.

CHRIS. I feel like all of you are out to *prove* something, to unmask some villain that isn't there.

SIHLE. Our imagination?

CHRIS. Precisely.

SIHLE. We've lived here two years, I'd like to be added to the group.

CHRIS. Now?

SIHLE. Yes, now, to the Stillwater update group.

CHRIS. You know, it's not a formal thing, we're not *plotting* or whatever you may think...

SIHLE. Then you wouldn't mind adding me.

CHRIS. Of course not, just, it was an oversight, this is silly all this fuss – while you? Fine, while you all wait, great.

CHRIS fiddles with his phone for a bit. Everyone waits. SIHLE gets out his phone. Waits too. It pings. He accepts the invite to join the group.

He looks at it for a bit. It pings many times. Lots of messages stream in.

SIHLE. Everyone's on here...

CHRIS. It was, like I said, an oversight.

SIHLE. The whole street's on here.

CHRIS. What do you want me to say? It all came together very quickly, the chat, people panicked when they heard in the nextneighbourhoodover how one shack, *one*, had spawned a dozen, and then two dozen, and when residents tried to sell their properties they couldn't move them on the market, no one wants to live next to a field of land invaders, even if it's a perfectly *nice* house, even if the invaders are perfectly *nice* people, because even if your property has increased in value, it's only called *profit* when you *sell*, and if you can't *sell* you're a *prisoner*. You're a prisoner with a good house, anyway, by the time I realised you weren't on the group, Sihle, it was too late and it would've been awkward for both of us.

SIHLE. An oversight.
You never changed your mind about me, did you? Since that first day you met me in the driveway.

SIHLE gets up.

I'm sorry, I won't sign this.

ANDREW. What the fuck's happening now?

SIHLE. It appears we're leaving.

JESS. (We haven't gotten through the agenda.)

LYNETTE. So you're not going to sign the...?

SIHLE. Bonolo? Ready?

SIHLE waits at the door.

But BONOLO *hasn't moved. She's only been listening very carefully. And considering. Her mouth is dry. Hearing her name surprises her.*

BONOLO. Ready...?

SIHLE. Are you ready to leave?

During the following bit, LYNETTE, CHRIS, JESS *and* ANDREW *stay on the stage, but the lights close in on* SIHLE *and* BONOLO *until it's just them two, outside of time.*

The others listen and watch from the darkness.

SIHLE *walks up to* BONOLO. *He whispers.* [*NO TRANSLATION IS PROVIDED.*]

Khumbula ukuthi awubonakali futhi uhamba kancane ukuze ungabavusi abalele. Ngezinye izikhathi kungcono kakhulu ukungabavusi; zimbalwa izinto emhlabeni eziyingozi njengabalala.

[*Remember to be invisible and move slowly so you don't wake them. Sometimes it is best not to wake them; few things in the world are as dangerous as sleepwalkers.*]

BONOLO *doesn't understand. She wrestles. She swallows. She can't make sense of it.*

BONOLO *reaches for the pen. She doesn't get up. Very measured, growing in conviction as she speaks:*

BONOLO. I apologise for Sihle's little outburst. We allowed ourselves to get emotional about this issue, I'm truly sorry. I totally understand where you're all coming from and it's fair. Your reaction, Andrew, is fair. Yours too Chris, you love this community. We **all** love this community. It comes from a place of love and of... needing to protect what we love.

The lights begin to open up again.

When we feel threatened, when our place in the world is
threatened, our instinct is to create an, an, opposition. To
create a 'we' so that there can be a 'them'. It's an instinct and
I understand it and I… while nobody enjoys being 'them',
I realise that I exist in this ecosystem… that I have a role to
play inside it. I am part of the 'we'. It was granted to me.
I chose it. And you can't be on both sides of that ecosystem.
Eventually you find your place. What Sihle's been telling me
is… you can't blame the 'we' for trying to protect what we
love. You can't blame **us**. So, my apologies. Let's wrap this up.

BONOLO *reads the eviction order out loud.*

'You are hereby requested to vacate the property within five
days or we will be forced to take legal…', blah blah, got it.
Signed: Bonolo Mbatha.'

She signs with a flourish.

She holds out the pen to SIHLE.

Sihle? Now you.

SIHLE *doesn't take the pen. Only stares at her. At the loaded
weapon, held out by* BONOLO.

He's furious. BONOLO'*s very calm.*

This is what you said it takes, isn't it?
For us to be part of Stillwater.
Sihle. That's whose side we're on.

The others all watch them, unmoving. SIHLE *doesn't reach
for the pen.*

As the lights begin to fade. Slip into:

Epilogue: Pepper Lane

A day in the past.

A differently composed LYNETTE *enters from outside.*

As this scene continues, BONOLO *and* SIHLE*'s silhouettes are seen framing the shack. Looking at it.*

LYNETTE. Sorry about that.

JESS. Oh no trouble, we were just admiring.

LYNETTE. I just had to see them off.

JESS. Lovely family.

ANDREW. Cute kids.

LYNETTE. Sweet, aren't they? Dear people. And they speak such good English! Anyway – now you're back where you started.

Garden door out to the left, sliding windows are newly installed and as you can see, plenty of natural light. And that's the grand tour. Any questions?

ANDREW. No.

JESS. It's gorgeous here.

LYNETTE. Isn't it?

ANDREW. Spacious. It's shocking how much space there is.

JESS. I see it. My studio, right here, looking out this big window, at that beautiful patch of open land. That stray piece over there's big enough to turn into a vegetable garden. The couches in kind of a semicircle –

ANDREW. Let's not get ahead of ourselves.

JESS. Organic vegetables. (Let me dream, babe?), muted colour palette.

LYNETTE. What a lovely idea, muted tones? I'd do the same, anything too loud gives me a headache. And this space is a blank canvas, your imagination is the limit here.

JESS. Well thanks for your time, Lynette. Really. We love the house, we'll… we'll be in touch about an offer.

LYNETTE. Uh-oh. I know that tone.

JESS. What'd you mean?

LYNETTE. It's the tone you use on call-centre people. 'Sorry, can't talk now, try me this evening.' When you have no intention of picking up the phone ever again.

ANDREW. *Noooo*.

LYNETTE. Yes. Absolutely, that's what it is.

ANDREW. We, just need some time to think. Three-point-five is a bit outside our –

JESS. It's not that we don't love it.

ANDREW. No, but it's outside the range we were shooting for.

LYNETTE. Sure, understandable. You had a budget in mind, this was slightly over –

ANDREW. That other couple offered three hundred thousand more. We eavesdropped in the bedroom.

LYNETTE. Is that so?

JESS. That's what we heard.

LYNETTE. Can I tell you both something? In confidence.

JESS. Of course.

LYNETTE. I really like you.

JESS. Well… thank you. We're flattered.

ANDREW. We like you too.

LYNETTE. And that counts for something.

ANDREW (*joking*). Currency?

LYNETTE. In a way. You could say currency.

ANDREW. What can we buy with it?

JESS. Babe.

LYNETTE. No, it's a perfectly good question. You can buy the house.

JESS. We can?

ANDREW. We can't. Jess, your father has been extremely generous, but three-point-five is a stretch, even for him. Two-point-eight is about as far as we can go.

LYNETTE. Then that's what you'll get it for.

    JESS, ANDREW *confused*.

ANDREW. Two-point-eight?

LYNETTE. Uh-huh.

JESS. That substantially reduces your commission, Lyn.

LYNETTE. I know. *I know.*

    Off their skepticism:

    When Chris and I – my husband, Chris – when we were starting out, young, in love, we were idealists. In fact, you remind me of us. Wide-eyed, a little afraid of the world, a little cautious. Life pushed us off the edge and Stillwater caught us. Gave us a solid footing. A foundation. Where you live becomes intimate, doesn't it? And who you live next door to. You want to share that space – your space – with people you can connect with, see yourself in. Have things in common with. Grow into. Grow with.

JESS. Sure you do.

LYNETTE. And you are those people. So I'm saying, it's not about the money. It's about community. If you like it here –

JESS. We love it here.

LYNETTE. I'm so pleased. It's a good neighbourhood, isn't it?

JESS. It really is. And this is a good house.

JESS *turns to* ANDREW, *grins*.

Ours?

ANDREW. Ours.

JESS *embraces* ANDREW *while* LYNETTE *looks on as –*

The shack begins to change now.

BONOLO *is seen back there, in silhouette, taking it apart with her hands.*

Taking off its chimney. Taking off its roof.

Dismantling its door.

Removing a window.

Taking the thing apart like a children's toy, like something made of Lego, piece by piece, wall by wall.

SIHLE *is there too. He watches her while she does it. Until, eventually, there's nothing left.*

Only them.

A Nick Hern Book

A Good House first published as a paperback original in Great Britain in 2025 by Nick Hern Books Limited, The Glasshouse, 49a Goldhawk Road, London W12 8QP, in association with the Royal Court Theatre, London, and Bristol Old Vic

A Good House © 2025 Amy Jephta

Amy Jephta has asserted her right to be identified as the author of this work

Cover artwork: Guy J Sanders

Designed and typeset by Nick Hern Books, London
Printed in the UK by by CPI Group (UK) Ltd

A CIP catalogue record for this book is available from the British Library

ISBN   978 1 83904 421 2

www.nickhernbooks.co.uk

@nickhernbooks